LINCOLN CHRISTIAN COLLEGE AND SEMINARY

SEIZING THE TORCH

LINCOLN CHRISTIAN COLLEGE AND SEMINARY

SEIZING
THE
TORCH

*Leadership
for a New
Generation*

TED W.
ENGSTROM
AND
ROBERT C.
LARSON

GL
Regal Books
A Division of GL Publications
Ventura, California, U.S.A.

Published by Regal Books
A Division of GL Publications
Ventura, California 93006
Printed in U.S.A.

Unless otherwise indicated, Scripture quotations are from the *New King James Version, Holy Bible.* Copyright © 1979, 1980, 1982 by Thomas Nelson Inc., Publishers. Used by permission.
Also quoted are:
KJV—*Authorized King James Version*
RSV—From *Revised Standard Version* of the Bible, copyrighted 1946 and 1952 by the Division of Christian Education of the NCCC, U.S.A., and used by permission.
TLB—from *The Living Bible,* Copyright © 1971 by Tyndale House Publishers, Wheaton, Illinois. Used by permission.

© Copyright 1988 by Ted W. Engstrom
All rights reserved.

Any omission of credits or permissions granted is unintentional. The publisher requests documentation for future printings.

Library of Congress Cataloging-in-Publication Data

Engstrom, Theodore Wilhelm, 1916-
    Seizing the torch : leadership for a new generation / by Ted W. Engstrom,
with Robert C. Larson.
        p.   cm.
    Bibliography: p.
    ISBN 0-8307-1195-3
    1. Christian leadership. I. Larson, Robert C. II. Title.
BV652.1.E54 1988
253—dc19   88-10159
                                                                                CIP

1 2 3 4 5 6 7 8 9 10/ 91 90 89 88

Rights for publishing this book in other languages are contracted by Gospel Literature International (GLINT) foundation. GLINT also provides technical help for the adaptation, translation, and publishing of Bible study resources and books in scores of languages worldwide. For further information, contact GLINT, Post Office Box 488, Rosemead, California, 91770, U.S.A., or the publisher.

CONTENTS

Gratis

96242

INTRODUCTION

*"Teach these great truths to trustworthy
men who will, in turn, pass them
on to others."*
2 Timothy 2:2, *The Living Bible*

Out of my years of experience with Youth for Christ, I developed a deep appreciation for young leadership. And while I thought I'd seen the best in those early years, I'm now even more impressed with the quality, dedication, ability and multi-ranged skills of today's young leaders.

In spite of the seemingly insurmountable problems that beset our families, our society and our age, today's young leaders have proven they have the guts, determination, growing maturity and spirit to turn this world around for Jesus Christ. It's my prayer and sincerest hope that this book will encourage them to "seize the torch" of leadership responsibility as never before. I pray it will galvanize their thinking about their faith and ever-shrinking world as they deal with qualities as important today as when I began my ministry over half a century ago, qualities such as commitment, goal setting, motivation, enthusiasm, honesty, courage, decision making, responsibility and the ability to prioritize. These are the qualities upon which Robert C. Larson and I have built this book, because they are the stuff today's leaders must develop to be all they can be.

The twenty-first century is right around the corner. Not long ago I, too, stood at the threshold of a new epoch. It wasn't the entrance into a new century. Rather it was the passage into a bright new world of hope and ambition at the end of World War II. It only seemed like a new century—bright as a mint-fresh penny. A civilized world had marched home triumphantly with the realization we had physically conquered the forces of darkness; and a great number of us wanted to march back and conquer that same world spiritually.

Dawson Trotman remembered the platoons of U.S. soldiers all over the world who saluted our Lord and Master. To mobilize their zeal, he organized a group called the Navigators.

Torrey Johnson observed young people who were passionate for change. He formed Youth for Christ.

Billy Graham was so enthusiastic and effective that publisher William Randolph Hearst urged editors to "puff Graham."

Back then none of us lacked commitment for Christ, but we all lacked training for the burdens leadership demanded. Now after 40 years of trial and error, I have come to understand leadership much better. But since it's too late for me to start over, the best I can do is pass on to my readers what I feel I have learned.

The choices are much harder today. At the close of WWII, we all knew who the enemy was. We shared the same experiences—the victories and the defeats. We all belonged to the winning team. Somehow it was easier to face the new missionary challenges with confidence. Today the Western world cannot agree on who the enemy is. And no one really feels like an international winner. No wonder many young people find it difficult to commit to Christian leadership.

But we cannot afford to wait until the days of victory after the next world war to spark us into action. Forty years ago we had a common cause for missionary zeal, but little leadership experience. Today we seem to lack shared purpose and cause, but are enriched with four decades of leadership experience for Christ.

I invite you to tear into this book and use it, or simply tear it in two and walk away. The time for disinterest and faintheartedness is past. After all, how much more pollution, crime, violence, promiscuity, toxic waste, disease, hatred, nuclear stockpiles and Satanism will God allow to disgrace His handiwork?

It's taken me and my colleagues 40 years to relearn the wisdom of the ages. Today's young leaders can't afford to wait that long.

Our energetic, young pioneers standing on the threshold of the twenty-first century have so much to offer. I pray they will take up the challenge outlined in these chapters and run—for their sake, and for the sake of those who already look to them for leadership.

Chapter One

COMMITMENT
What Are You Willing to Die For?

Many leaders today think Christian service is an easy way to achieve comfort and financial security. Mistake! Christianity is not Wall Street. It's "will street."

*"For I am ready
not only to be bound,
but also to die at Jerusalem
for the name of the Lord Jesus."*
Acts 21:13

L ook at the torch!" screamed untold thousands during
the 1984 Olympic Torch relay across America.
Remember when 4,000 runners carried an official flame
from New York to Los Angeles over a 9,000-mile course?
I can still feel the chill running down my spine as Rafer
Johnson ran up those long steps and finally transferred his
flame from Mount Olympia to the Los Angeles Coliseum.
What a sense of participation, unity and completion.

"Look at the torch," shouted the same international
crowd when Lady Liberty showed us her new golden
flame at the centennial celebration of the Statue of Liberty
on July 4, 1986.

There's something hypnotic about fire. Especially one
that has endured the hardships of time and distance to
burn brightly and faithfully.

This book is about yet another torch. One which has
been handed off in a solemn relay for nearly 2,000 years.

"You are the light of the world," Christ told the original disciples in Matthew 5:14. "Let your light so shine before men, that they may see your good works and glorify your Father in heaven" (v. 16).

I've met a lot of "torches" in my time. Christians, both men and women, of all colors, and languages, whose burning passion was to glorify their Father. They've ignited me, and I'm confident they can do the same for you.

THE FIRES OF COMMITMENT

I can only imagine how the conversation might have gone back in 1947 when Bob Pierce announced to his father-in-law he wanted to leave the family ministry and become a missionary to China.

"Papa Johnson, you've given me such a good opportunity to build a secure and comfortable life here at home that I want to give it all up, go into debt and move to China." You can be certain he didn't say it that way. But that's how it might have sounded to everyone else who didn't understand Bob's fire of commitment.

His understanding of this vital resource resulted in the formation of World Vision International in California. Bob is but one of hundreds of luminaries in a night sky filled with Christian "lights."

I was privileged to cut my leadership teeth with a group of young men who didn't know the meaning of *can't.* These men were willing, perhaps unwisely at times, to leave their families, their jobs, even their congregations to step out in bold, reckless faith. Torrey Johnson, the founder of Youth for Christ, left his well-established church for another flock in need of a shepherd. Jim Rayburn sold out of his successful business interests to invest in Young Life. Bob Evans was a Navy chaplain who dared to call on new ports in his desire to bring the gospel to Europe.

Here was commitment. And I was learning from it.

The whole world was our congregation. A group of visionaries in the Philippines started a ministry that has continued to jolt those scattered islands. Far East Broadcasting Company with Bob Bowman, Bill Roberts and John Broger started about that same time—soon after WWII when the need for change was obvious to everyone and so was the need for committed leaders.

I remember a youth congress in Bristol, England, where we worked with what we called "Teddy Boys." The Teddy Boys were delinquents, and we'd work half the night at a big rally in the stadium. Then we'd go out on the streets and into the pubs to share, witness, sing and testify. This would usually go on well into the night, sometimes until four in the morning. And nobody got all that worried about his own needs.

That's where we met the pink-haired prostitute. Some of our folks witnessed to her and within 48 hours she was transformed. She changed her whole demeanor and appearance and started coming to our meetings. She didn't miss a service. She began to testify to other prostitutes and the Teddy Boys she knew. We followed her progress for years through regular Bible school—all because a few members of our group had the commitment and leadership to push on relentlessly for yet another restless soul.

Our messages were simple yet profound. John 3:16, Romans 3 and 4—basic gospel messages focusing on the way of salvation. That was always the theme. The driving motivation back then was to bring people to faith in Christ. We didn't talk very much about "discipleship;" we concentrated on soul winning and witnessing.

If Jesus were to appear as an adjunct professor at an

evangelical seminary today, I believe He'd be a professor of New Testament preaching. He'd talk about His relationship with His Father. I think His sermons would be simple. You'd hear the message to Nicodemus—"You must be born again" (see John 3:3). That message has never lost its life.

This clarity of vision served well in the past. It will do the same for up-and-coming leaders.

WHY COMMITMENT?

What is there about the quality of commitment that makes it such a powerful ally of leadership?

Young leaders today are filled with commitment. But the environment in which they must lead demands a crash course in how to work with the so-called "yuppie mentality."

Meet the pig in a python. That's the name some demographers have given to the vast swell of post-WWII babies as they move through the snake of time. And all along the way many of these 76 million Americans born between 1946 and 1964 have behaved much like selfish pigs. From their silver spoons as infants to their silver and gold pen sets as young upwardly mobile professionals, this group has, for the most part, thought more of security than salvation.

They're committed to a set of personal goals such as cars, appliances, wardrobe, travel, entertainment, etc., but tragically they are a "generation that has avoided or postponed commitment to others" according to a probing cover story by *Time* magazine.[1]

"Many have little loyalty to their employers and less to political leaders or ideas. Partly because of the economic squeeze, they get married later and have children later.

They also divorce more than their parents."[2]

Young people of the "Now" generation are growing into middle-aged adults of the "what now?" generation.

In my mind, the only meaningful answer to what now? is service and commitment.

X-RAY OF A LEADER

Before we look more closely at the workings of commitment, I'd like to step back and cast some light on the broader subject of leadership.

How can you recognize a leader? Do leaders have louder voices for ordering people around? Or larger biceps for strong-arming their followers. How easy it would be for everyone if we could spot a leader by physical appearances alone. The descendants of King Saul would still be ruling over Israel and David's father would never have permitted Samuel to anoint the "runt" of his family as leader of the nation (see 1 Sam. 16:6-13).

But since we cannot look on the outward appearance for an accurate assessment of leadership abilities, let's peer into the inner being for positive identification.

Notice how the head is well-stocked with goals and plans for the organization. The neck is quite agile with no signs of stiffness. It easily bends to the forces above it. The shoulders are square and firm with plenty of room for responsibility. The right arm is skilled at organization while the left arm knows how to delegate and let go. The right leg leads with drive and initiative while the left leg follows through with persistence and perseverance. Our X-ray also reveals a well developed heart and lungs full of spirit. Notice how these vital organs are protected by strong ribs of character, willpower and discipline. The entire skeleton is symetrically attached to a straight and firm backbone.

Such characteristics cannot be seen from the outside. But with this book, you will begin to recognize these inner strengths by the outward shadow they cast through deeds, actions, results and Christian fruit. The more you understand about the skeleton beneath an effective leader, the more you'll understand about strengthening these abilities in yourself and in others.

TRAITS OF A LEADER IN ACTION

Some leadership traits won't show up on a still-frame X-ray because you have to see them in action to know they're present. Like blood pressure testing or an EKG, many aspects of leadership are best observed in motion. The following traits mark the difference between a leader who stands up under the load, and a leader who takes up the challenge and runs.

First is *enthusiasm*. This trait includes both optimism and hope. No pessimist has ever made a great leader. The pessimist sees a difficulty in every opportunity; the optimist sees an opportunity in every difficulty. Enthusiasm conveys this hope and faith to everyone else.

A second trait is *trustworthiness*. A Christian leader is honest and transparent in all dealings and relationships. A leader must be worthy of trust. Here is a person of integrity and someone whose word is sure.

Third, the spiritual leader is *disciplined*. Someone who has conquered self wins respect and cooperation from others. An effective leader will work while others waste time, study while others sleep, pray while others play.

Fourth, a leader has *confidence*. If a leader does not believe in his or her own decisions, how will anyone else?

A fifth trait is *decisiveness*. When all the facts are in, a swift and clear decision is the mark of a true leader. The person at the helm will resist the temptation to procrastinate in reaching a decision, and will not vacillate after a decision has been made. Indecision in a time of emergency destroys the capacity to lead.

Sixth, *courage* marks strong leadership. Courage of the highest order is demanded of the spiritual leader. The greatest degree of courage is seen in the person who is most fearful but refuses to capitulate to the fear. However fearful they might have been, God's leaders in every generation have been commanded to "be of good courage" (see Josh. 1:6). When everyone else has fled, courage is the capacity to stay in there five minutes longer! It's as if success relied less on ability and more on durability. We'll have a great deal more to say about courage in chapter 6.

A seventh vital trait of leadership is *humor*. This is expressed in the ability to see the funny or strange side of life. It is reported that Admiral Chester W. Nimitz, upon viewing the devastation of Kwajalein after a battle in WWII, remarked to his staff, "It's the worst devastation I've ever seen except for that last Texas picnic in Honolulu." A good leader knows the value of a contagious smile.

A further trait of leadership is *loyalty*, expressed in constancy, steadfastness and faithfulness. A lack of loyalty to leadership will destroy an organization. As the group must be loyal to the leader, that chief, in turn, must be loyal to them.

A final trait, though many more could be added, is *unselfishness*. This is demonstrated by the leader who can forget personal needs in the interest of others. Self-preservation is acknowledged to be the first law of nature, but it's been said that self-sacrifice remains the greatest rule of grace.

Leadership does not come naturally for most. Nor does leadership come in "Ten Easy Steps." Therefore, potential leaders need to learn the techniques and develop traits that will enhance their effectiveness for leadership. Merely emulating someone else will not do.

PEOPLE WANT TO BE LED, NOT MANAGED

Although I've written a number of books on management, this is not a management text. This is a book about leadership—passing the torch on to our new leaders, who will help take us into the next century.

People want regular contact with a caring, feeling leader instead of impersonal manipulation from a cold manager.

One of the quickest ways I know of to lose control of a group is to confuse leadership with management. People expect someone to manage things and situations, but they personally want to be led. Let's take a look at some of the distinctions between leadership and management that will help encourage and motivate your followers.

1. *Leadership is an art; management is a science.* Good management puts sheet music in front of the orchestra. But it takes a conductor to lead the musicians to greatness.

2. *Leadership sees the destination; management oversees the journey.* How often do we become so concerned about shoveling coal into the boilers that we forget to steer the ship?

3. *Leadership creates thought; management creates action.* Action is important as long as we remember why we're doing what we're doing in the first place.

4. *Leadership exercises faith; management deals with works.* Someone must believe a project is worthwhile and possible, before anyone else will even try.

5. *Leadership seeks results (at any price); management seeks efficiency.* Trailblazing, is never easy. Pioneers are the last to find the shortcut. But without the pathfinders we would have no need of road builders.

6. *Leadership makes things happen; management keeps them happening.* Loading fuel on a roaring fire is markedly different than coaxing an ember into a blaze.

7. *Leadership starts new projects; management finishes old ones.* Here's where the discipline of a good manager helps control the overzealous leader. For example, it does no good to launch into a new fund-raising project if the old one hasn't gone far enough to show whether it is working or not.

Leadership and management work hand in glove. But my experience has shown that people want regular contact with a caring, feeling leader instead of impersonal manipulation from a cold manager.

This does not mean that leaders are better than managers. I take great satisfaction in my accomplishments over the years as a manager. But what these distinctions do tell us is that both roles are important and we'd best not confuse the two, or omit either one.

Later, as more clues about Christian leadership unfold throughout this book, you will understand how to apply these distinctions and make the necessary changes to become a more effective leader. This knowledge holds great promise for every aspect of life; church, family, business and whatever area you wish to improve.

THE ONE SINGLE QUALITY

With this grand overview of leadership, we are better prepared to appreciate the contribution of *commitment*.

I'm convinced that unswerving commitment to a person, cause or an idea is the one single quality that produces a leader. When someone drives self and personal resources toward an "impossible" goal against overwhelming odds, other people begin to follow.

In 1858 a small, frail lad was born to a rich family in New York. Along with feeble eyesight, he suffered from asthma so badly that at times he couldn't blow out the bedside candle. But none of this stopped him from becoming one of the most powerful men on earth.

Theodore Roosevelt's father called Teddy aside when he was 11 or 12 and told him that a good mind alone would not ensure success—he must build himself a powerful new body to match it. Theodore did so, spending thousands of hours chinning himself, lifting weights and rattling a punching bag. Little wonder he rose like a rocket in the world of politics: elected to the New York legislature at 23; candidate for mayor at 28; U.S. Civil Service Commissioner under two presidents; president of the police commission of New York; national hero as leader of the Rough Riders in the Spanish-American War at 40; then, in just three busy years, governor of New York, vice president, then President. In 1905 Teddy Roosevelt received the Nobel Peace Prize for his efforts in helping to end the Russo-Japanese war. At 5 foot 9, TR was a small man made large through commitment.[3]

COMMITMENT VERSUS FAILURE

Successful leaders are usually endowed with enough

excuses to satisfy a thousand failures. But commitment drives them on.

Thomas Edison dreamed of a lamp that would help people see by means of the invisible force of electricity. He could have quit and no one would have blamed him. After all, he had felt the sting of failure more than 10,000 times in that one project alone. Chances are, you and I haven't had that many failures during our combined lifetimes.

"He possesses minimal football knowledge. Lacks motivation," an expert once said of Vince Lombardi. "Can't act! Slightly bald! Can dance a little!" read Fred Astaire's first screen test in 1933. Referring to Albert Einstein, someone quipped, "He doesn't wear socks and forgets to cut his hair. Could be mentally retarded." I'm sure these remarks hurt them as deeply as they would hurt us. But true leadership is never held back by mere opinion.

The Wright brothers decided they wanted to do more than repair bikes in their Dayton, Ohio bicycle shop. They dreamed of a machine that could ride the sky. People laughed at them. Some said it was not God's will for men to fly. But Orville and Wilbur determined to follow their star. They persisted with their dream. Then, on December 17, 1903 near Kitty Hawk, North Carolina, the first power-driven airplane roared into history.

Daniel Webster could not make a speech until he spent years of disciplined effort. Finally, he became one of America's greatest orators.

George Washington lost more battles than he won. But his victories were lasting ones.

Extraordinary feats of superhumans? No, these are the attainable accomplishments of everyday people like you and me who worked on their dream until what they knew was possible became clear to everyone else.

But success required determination.

John Bunyan wrote *Pilgrim's Progress* while languishing in Bedford prison in England, locked up for his vocal views on religion.

Helen Keller was stricken deaf, blind and dumb soon after birth. Did she quit? Hardly. Her name already stands alongside those of the most respected people in history. She knew what courage and discipline were all about. It's called commitment.

Charles Dickens began his illustrious career with the unimpressive job of pasting labels on blacking pots. The tragedy of his first love shot through to the depths of his soul, touching off a genius of creativity that made him one of the greatest authors of all time.

Robert Burns was an illiterate country boy; O. Henry, a criminal and an outcast; Beethoven was deaf; poet John Milton was blind. But once they mastered their own weaknesses and committed themselves to service, they inspired us all.

Commitment, even at its struggling, most fledgling level, contributes to personal growth and enhances our capacity to grow even more.

Yes, their names are world renowned today, but they were everyday unknowns before their commitment became clear to others.

If these leaders were able to tap the power of commitment for meeting their physical goals, how much more should we be able to harness this force for meeting our spiritual goals? Perhaps people would show a great deal more interest in commitment to God and Christ if they had a better understanding of the benefits involved.

RESULTS YOU CAN SEE

The first, and perhaps most obvious, result of our commitment to a loving God is *personal growth*. It's been said that God's reward for a job well done is in giving us a bigger job to do. It's the same with commitment. Commitment, even at its struggling, most fledgling level, contributes to personal growth and enhances our capacity to grow even more.

Internal peace that results from a decision is another by-product of commitment. Be hot or cold, but not in-between. There is no peace in indecision. These words from my book *A Time for Commitment* say it well: "On the beach of hesitation bleach the bones of countless millions who sat down to wait, and waiting, died."⁴ Ever wonder why the big fish vomited out Jonah? The disobedient preacher was *lukewarm*! Commitment and lukewarmness fly in the face of each other. Commitment and a deep sense of internal peace go hand in hand.

When you commit yourself to God and to His plans, there is yet a third result. *Your life takes on purpose.* You discover a reason for living. Suddenly, you are more than flesh and bone. You are a person of destiny and purpose. You begin to echo the words of the poet, Goethe, who said, "Knowing is not enough; we must apply. Willing is not enough; we must do." And you begin to *do it* with an enthusiasm and desire you never had before. Why? Because you are living out your God-ordained design for commitment. You are making commitment work for you.

Often we hear people say, "I'm unhappy," as if happiness were somehow supposed to be the ultimate purpose of life. I've found it's just the opposite. Usually I'm happiest when I'm not even thinking about being happy. Happiness and joy are always by-products of my commitment to a task, a person, an idea. It often comes in the midst of intense struggle—even pain. But without question my greatest happiness comes in service to others and in commiting myself to people, projects and plans.

Consider what my friend, Charles "Tremendous" Jones has to say. "Work as hard as you can, get as much as you can, give as much as you can." That's happiness. That's commitment.

NON-KOSHER COMMITMENT

Perhaps you've heard the story of the chicken and the pig. The two were walking side by side along a country road when they noticed an announcement tacked on the bulletin board of a little country church. The sign read: Ham and Eggs breakfast this Sunday at 7:30 A.M. All are invited.

The pig turned to the chicken and said, "Will you look at that! For you, that's no more than a day's work. But for me, it's total commitment!"

I can understand the pig's reaction. Commitment *is* total involvement. Women can't get partially pregnant. And leaders can't succeed with partial commitment.

HOW TO DIE FOR THE CAUSE— AND LIVE TO SERVE AGAIN

What kind of commitment is expected from a Christian leader? How can you demonstrate a willingness to die for the Lord and still live long enough to serve your fellowman?

"Greater love has no man than this, than to lay down one's life for his friends," Christ reminded us in John

15:13. But was He only referring to a single act of heroism such as running into a burning building or pulling someone out of the deep? How else can we lay down our life?

Paul speaks of mortifying the "deeds of the body," and presenting yourself as a "living sacrifice." In speaking of the battle he waged against the pulls of the carnal flesh he remarked, "I die daily" (see Rom. 8:13, Rom. 12:1, 1 Cor. 15:31).

Here then is one of the first life-and-death commitments a Christian leader has to make. Selfish desires cry out for satisfaction. Are we willing to put them to death and surrender our life to the Master?

But beware! Three cancerous parasites are waiting to devour the Spirit-led Christian. The apostle John warns us in 1 John 2:16. We have to mortify "the lust of the flesh, the lust of the eyes, and the pride of life" before they rise up and consume us.

Of these, pride is the most insidious. A leader must die to pride and personal ambition. One thing that will hurt a young person in the ministry faster than anything else is setting *personal* (self-inspired) goals rather than listening to the voice of the Spirit. Personal ambition can be dangerous.

Ironically, those who dedicate themselves to Christ often discover that people want to worship them instead of God. A leader must die to adulation. A public figure, whether the President of the United States, the pastor of a large church, an evangelist or a youth worker often feeds on the good things people say when face-to-face. On the other hand, the remarks spoken behind their back could make them gag. And sadly, some Christian leaders have fixed their commitment on this handful of empty wind.

Second, we have to die to the dollar sign, the "lust of the eyes." Many leaders today think Christian service is an easy way to achieve comfort and financial security. Mistake! Christianity is not Wall Street. It's "will street."

And finally, John warns against loose morals, the "lust of the flesh." Searching for a ready, willing body will never lead to an able spirit.

It all boils down to one simple decision. Are you willing to slay the selfish self to serve?

That reminds me of one of the first episodes of a recently new network TV program called "Amen." On the show the pastor had quit. Now the deacons were interviewing the Reverend Reuben Gregory for the position. Somebody asked about his educational background and the Reverend replied, "I have a Bachelor of Arts degree from Morehouse College, a Master of Religious Education from the Yale Divinity School and I have a Doctorate in Christian Studies from the Union Theological Seminary." To which a deacon replied, "Yeah, but do you believe in God?"

TWELVE TRENDS CHALLENGING TODAY'S LEADERS

If committing yourself to the role of a dedicated Christian leader seems difficult, congratulations. You're well on your way toward progress. It would be oh so easy to turn aside to a selfish life of endive salad, designer running shoes, and a personal cappuccino machine.

But outside the world is crying for leadership. Let's take a look at some of the pressing issues that plead in the decades ahead for you to master the skills of a committed leader.

1. Despite an increase in the visible role of religion, Christian values are having less impact on society than ever before. Since the 1960s church membership and attendance have remained static. But in practice the

supernatural is less plausible to most today than in earlier generations.

2. Christian groups are permitting their tensions and differences to polarize and fragment their impact. Evangelicals are moving more aggressively into the political sphere. They find themselves involved in issues of ethical concern as never before—abortion, women's roles and economic life-styles. These trends have weakened the unified witness to secular society.

3. Growing poverty at home and abroad is requiring the Church to review its message and methods of charity. The gap between affluent nations and emerging ones widens with each decade. Today 1 billion people—one-fifth of the world's family—are undernourished. This increase in poverty is making some non-Christian ideologies more attractive than traditional Christianity. Unless the Church addresses wealth and poverty in the context of the gospel, then Marxism, liberation theology and socialism may increasingly be accepted as alternatives to a Bible-based faith.

4. The gulf between evangelicals and mainline social/ political action groups has narrowed. Now many different groups and factions are competing for the loyalty of the same believers.

5. The aging of the North American population plus changing immigration patterns are dramatically altering the ministry and responsibility of the Church. Longevity is increasing the portion of elderly in American society. Retirement will probably move to age 70 or 75. Care of the aged is becoming increasingly big business. In addition, the baby boom of previous years is now reaching its career peak, symbolized by "yuppie" values and goals. The emerging Hispanic minority plus the influx of Asian immigrants will figure in the strategic plans of all denomina-

tions. Each of these groups is a challenge to ministry and evangelism hitherto unknown. Urbanization will particularly affect the evangelical church, which has its highest percentage of members in rural communities.

6. Women are assuming a more prominent leadership role in society and in the Church. As growing numbers of women assume management positions in the workplace, we can expect a noticeable arrival of women in church leadership and Christian organization management. In society at large, the ability of women to regulate their procreative life is having an immense impact on how women live and work. Women will experience both increasing freedom of choice and increasing stress in their marriages and the structure of the family unity. The Church will increasingly find its volunteer work force, nonworking females, diminished in numbers as more and more women opt for working outside the home.

7. New technology will change our work and leisure. Major changes in economics and employment will reshape the way we live. High tech is moving us rapidly toward new life-styles. The rise of the computer brings with it the potential to work at home, with electronic networks for travel, trading, shopping, banking and electronic mail. Cable television promises the opportunity for education in the home. Robotics is changing the face of the assembly line, giving less desirable jobs to machines while it redirects people into more technical, information-oriented, managerial types of work. Unemployment will increase.

8. The charismatic movement will continue to be the fastest growing segment of the Church. This seems to be true, not only in America, but worldwide. It's especially true of individual charismatic churches, even where denominational growth has slowed.

9. Mainline denominations, including such groups as

the Southern Baptists, Lutherans, Presbyterians and the Roman Catholics, are undergoing a period of stress, tension and shifting of power of enormous proportions. This is due to a variety of organizational, sociopolitical, geographic and ideological factors. In general, national power is being deferred to regional and local bodies. Denominational ties will continue to be less and less important to individual churches and church members.

10. The search for self-fulfillment through self-centered activities will increasingly prove to be self-destructive. Despite the growing secularization of society and the attraction of materialism, people will still value personal aspects of their lives—self-fulfillment, health and family. But in their headlong rush for self-fulfillment, people will sacrifice family or moral values, accepting a greater tolerance for sexual openness. This in turn will bring increased family disintegration, divorce and sexual activity outside marriage. This misguided search will continue to create intense frustration.

11. In an increasingly unstable world community, with the arms race continuing and the threat of nuclear war remaining, the average standard of living even in relatively well-off countries will continue to decline. Since the Church is generally supported by the discretionary income of its members, it will face declining income and financial support. Missions support will also be affected, as will nations able, or willing, to accept missionaries. The Church's message will also be influenced by its need to speak to the threat of nuclear war and the new balance of world finances.

12. The negative effect of media values on traditional American life will continue. Not only will TV, radio, cable television and films continue to preach non-Christian values, but society will continue to move in the direction of a

visual rather than a literate society. America's educators now grapple with the frustration that one in five cannot read. In a world that doesn't read, the Bible will continue to decline in influence.

Like teeth on a dragon, these are but part of the menace. Elsewhere in this book, you will see many other obstacles that defy common knowledge and cry out for uncommon leadership.

Several years ago, the *Global Prayer Digest* released a sobering statistic. Ninety percent of those who volunteer to become missionaries never go.[5]

Maybe conditions in their life changed. Maybe the work was too lengthy or too far away. Maybe they couldn't afford it. Or maybe they weren't committed.

WHAT HAVE WE SEEN?

1. *Seize the Torch.* The example of earlier Christians lights the way for us today. Men such as Bob Pierce, Torrey Johnson and others help us keep a sure grip on the torch of truth.

2. *Understand the traits of leadership.* Enthusiasm, trustworthiness, discipline, confidence, decisiveness, courage, humor, loyalty and unselfishness all prepare us for leadership and commitment.

3. *Look for thrilling results.* Commitment to Christ not only makes us more productive, but more happy and joyous as well.

4. *Die for your commitment every day.* To be committed to Christ is to slay the selfish self to serve.

5. *Recognize needs.* At least a dozen powerful trends are contorting the Church today. Are you ready to shoulder

your share of the load on behalf of the Church? Are you ready for the challenges that lie ahead?

We've seen the torch go by at the 1984 Olympics. We've seen it renewed on the Statue of Liberty. Can we settle for anything less inspiring and motivational for the bright truth of God?

Leadership is not a comfortable luxury. It is a burning necessity. And once you have committed yourself to the reality of this truth, you're ready to set your sights on the tools we discuss in chapter 2.

Chapter Two

GOAL SETTING
Your Prologue to the Future

An individual can
create, execute and
modify personal goals
with impunity. But
orchestrating a team
requires greater goal-
setting skills from the
conductor.

"Ours is a world where people don't know what they want and are willing to go through hell to get it."

D. Marquis[1]

For 20 years I've helped conduct a program called "Managing Your Time." This is a two-day seminar that usually leaves people talking to themselves and liking what they say. The first day covers personal time management, the second, organizational management. It's all there: goals, priorities and planning.

During these sessions we explore the fact that time is life. But if we called it our seminar "Managing Your Life," few would show much interest. Yet when we offer to help people manage their time, almost everyone perks up. It's almost as if we want to treat time as a possession we own instead of a master we serve.

Time is a perpetual contradiction. It is free to all, but many people would pay richly to gain it back. We can quantify it through calendars, watches and the tides, but we cannot contain it. Time lingers painfully for the patient and races through the hands of the doctor. Time stands still in the universe as we glide by on a spinning planet.

Fifty-two weeks per year, 168 hours per week, 1,440 minutes per day, we all have the same amount of time. Presidents and paperboys alike have all the time there is. The only difference is how they use it. "Doest thou love life? Then don't squander time. For that's the stuff life's made of," observed Scottish poet and novelist Sir Walter Scott (1771-1832).

Christ gave the matter even more urgency when He said, "I must work the works of Him who sent Me while it is day; *the* night is coming when no one can work" (John 9:4). Look at everything He accomplished in only three and a half years. What Christ did in less than 1,300 days still affects what you and I do after more than 1,900 years.

We cannot escape the importance of time. But all too often we conduct our lives as if we had all the time in the world to catch a couple of movies, go shopping, decorate the house and then do something for the Lord—if He still needs it.

But time is what helps us arrive. Travel long enough in one direction and you'll get there. I've heard it said, "If you don't know where you're going, you'll probably end up someplace else." Nothing could be more certain when it comes to handing off the torch in this relay for Christ.

ANY DIRECTION WAS THE RIGHT DIRECTION

In the early days of my Christian service, any direction was the right direction. The world needed so much help it didn't seem to matter where we spent time with the torch. Wherever we went, there was always another group of people hungering for the Word of God.

I remember an article I wrote as a young GI in World

War II. It illustrates how even those who were trained to fight in the armies of this world still took an interest in making peace with God.

"Every Christian service man is shocked by the profanity, vile language, smutty stories, and loose living which are so prevalent in the armed forces. It seems that all the barriers are lowered, and the more blatantly vulgar a man can speak and think and be, the better soldier or sailor he thinks he is. Yet, I have found that under all of this show of bravado, these young men, all of them, have a deep longing for peace and satisfaction in their hearts . . . These boys are not gospel-hardened, as are so many in the pews of our churches today; rather, they are gospel hungry."[2]

Eventually each of us must choose a standard for selecting what deserves attention and why.

Later, acting upon the encouragement of local church leaders, I led the local "Youth for Christ" organization while they packed 6,000 teens into a civic auditorium night after night in Grand Rapids, Michigan—with help from a new young preacher named Billy Graham. This soon led to my participation in the first World Congress on Evangelism in Beatenburg, Switzerland, held in August 1948. Everywhere we turned, new avenues for effective evangelism stretched out before us.

But the same law that makes every direction the right direction can also make any direction the wrong one. Without purpose or plan, there's as much reason to go somewhere else than where you've chosen to go. People get selfish, because it's easy to get trapped by the familiar paths and thereby ignore new roads for opportunity. Eventually each of us must choose a standard for selecting what deserves attention and why.

Enter goal setting.

I'm convinced our first and highest goal must be pleasing God. Paul set the example by telling us, "I press on toward the goal for the prize of the upward call of God in Christ Jesus" (Phil. 3:14, *RSV*). But what is that goal? Is it an all time record offering for overseas evangelism? Is it a special donation for a new wing on the local church? Someone must make a mark on the map and convince everyone else this is the goal we should press on for.

To be effective, a goal must be specific and measurable. Vague goals such as to increase membership, or to preach the gospel won't do. An example of a specific goal might be to increase church membership by 100 before the end of the year. This is specific and measurable.

I've learned if you cannot describe your goals and write them down for tangible measurement, you'll never achieve them. But I've also learned the importance of being realistic. Overly optimistic goals only frustrate people through failure. And featherweight goals bring ridicule on the whole process by challenging people to do less than they might have otherwise accomplished, if left alone to spread their own wings. Effective leaders motivate the entire team to create and achieve productive goals.

Characteristics of an Effective Goal

The larger the organization, the greater the need for goals. An individual can create, execute and modify personal goals with impunity. But orchestrating a team requires greater goal-setting skills from the conductor.

To help keep organizations in productive harmony,

consider these seven characteristics of an effective goal:

1. A goal should be related in specific ways to the needs of the organization.

2. A goal should be achievable. Suppose a growth-minded pastor challenges each member of the congregation to bring five new people "next Sunday." That two or three percent of the people might be able to do this is believable, but not all of the congregation will be able to—particularly when the church could seat only one-quarter of them all if they came. This goal is unrealistic and thus fails to challenge. On the other hand, if the goal were for each member to bring *one,* that would be believable.

3. A goal should have a date when it will be accomplished. If people do not have a clear picture as to the time frame within which a goal lies, they have entirely different assumptions as to how urgent it is. Let's get in there and double our giving! doesn't mean much until someone says when and, of course, how.

4. A goal must be measurable. Everyone must be able to tell it has happened, that it has become a past event. If we don't make goals measurable, we will take away from people their sense of accomplishment. If the goal is "double the giving," we had better decide how much money this will produce.

5. A goal must be claimed by someone. What is everyone's business is no one's business. Someone must own and possess the goal. The question is not whether we all believe in the goal, but who believes in it enough to make it happen.

6. A goal must be supported by the necessary resources. We must have an understanding of what it's going to cost in money, facilities and other types of energy. And we must have these resources available. Too often,

Christian organizations begin with money when they should begin with goals. But the fact remains that if the people do not have the energy to carry it off, the goal will not become operational.

7. A goal has to be supported by a plan. The point here is that we must know how we plan to reach the goal. We must believe we can get "there" from "here," and have some understanding of which way the path will lead.

PLOTTING THE PLAN

You and I are future-directed beings. We plan on the basis of what we perceived in the past, then we try to project this understanding into the future. Except for the most simple, close-in projects, it is unlikely that our predictions about the future will be 100 percent right. Murphy's Law that states, "If something can go wrong, it probably will" is another way of saying there are so many possibilities something other than what we expected and hoped for will happen, that the probability of things happening our way is remote. Sometimes O'Toole's law is even more appropriate. He's the one who said, "Murphy was an optimist!" We all have days like that.

Planning is an attempt to move from now to then, to change things from the way things are to the way things ought to be.

Then some may ask, "If we can't be sure of the future, why plan?" We plan to improve the probability that what we believe should happen will happen. The point of the planning arrow figuratively touches the goal. The steps that need to be accomplished stretch back along the arrow into the present to create a plan.

Four important links in the planning chain that I've identified over the years include:

1. Planning is a process. Like meal preparation or housecleaning, you cannot do it once and walk away forever. Between the time your plans are conceived and the first step is taken, change occurs. All planning needs a re-evaluation or feedback process that re-examines the future at each step and then measures the extent of the program. Some evaluation procedures are almost as intricate as the plan itself. Others are little more than the simple question, How are we doing? But the important thing to remember is to keep on planning.

2. Planning takes time. Sixty seconds of thought before dashing out the door can save hours of time in returning for something you forgot. Evaluation is worth every minute. But most of us won't do it unless we consciously set time aside to do so. A daily time to make up a things-to-do-list should be a habit. Setting times for monthly, quarterly and yearly review on our calendars will build the process into the regular work we need to do each day.

Because planning takes time, it should begin as far in advance as possible. In a church, why wait until October to start planning for the next year? The process should begin no later than April or May, so that as many people as possible can be brought in and no one is rushed into the future.

3. Planning is both personal and organizational. Many are misled into believing that planning for tomorrow is useful only for groups. To be truly effective, goal setting and planning must become a personal style of life. There is a direct relationship between a leader's organizational effectiveness and personal effectiveness. Both require planning.

4. Planning to fail. Many leaders are planning to fail by simply failing to plan, for two reasons. First, planning

rarely falls into the category of emergency and therefore does not appear to be urgent. It was President Eisenhower who reminded us that the important is seldom urgent. For example, it's urgent that you add oil to the car tomorrow if the warning light comes on to remind you. But it's more important that you send an invitation to a local VIP who needs enough time to consider attending the charity banquet you're coordinating in three months. But this takes planning, and so we easily fall prey to procrastination. Second, leaders usually consider themselves people of action. Planning, for many of them, is too slow a process, and they become impatient with details. They want to get on with the job without giving enough time and study to analyze the best way to accomplish it.

These problems can be alleviated if leaders will set a goal for themselves of setting goals. A few minutes for goal setting every day, in the morning or at the close of working hours, becomes a highly profitable discipline. Some people fear this process will confine and restrict them. On the contrary. Managing yourself is simply being a good steward of your time, talent and treasures.

MUCH ADO ABOUT "TO DO"

Most students of management are familiar with the classic—but can't be repeated too often—incident regarding the payment of a large sum of money for one simple goal-setting idea. For those who may not have chanced upon the story, it is well worth reviewing.

When Charles M. Schwab was president of U.S. Steel, he confronted Ivy Lee, a management consultant, with an unusual challenge: "Show me a way to get more things done," he demanded. "If it works, I'll pay anything within reason."

Lee handed Schwab a piece of paper. "Write down the things you have to do tomorrow," he said. Schwab did it. "Now number these items in the order of their real importance," Lee continued. Schwab did that too. "The first thing tomorrow morning," Lee added, "start working on number one and stay with it until it is completed. Next take number two and don't go any further until it is completed. Then proceed to number three, and so on. If you can't complete everything on schedule, don't worry. At least you will have taken care of the most important things before getting distracted by items of lesser consequence.

"The secret is to do this daily," continued Lee. "Evaluate the relative importance of the things you have to get done . . . establish priorities . . . record your plan of action . . . and stick to it. Do this every working day. After you have convinced yourself of the value of this system, have your men try it. Test it as long as you like. Then send me a check for whatever you think the idea is worth."[3]

In a few weeks Charles Schwab sent Ivy Lee a check for twenty-five thousand dollars. Schwab later said this lesson was the most profitable one he had ever learned in his business career.

Yet with all this writing about lists, Alan Lakein makes an incisive observation in his highly acclaimed book, *How to Get Control of Your Time and Your Life.* "Again and again when I talked to successful businessmen and government administrators, the *To Do* list came up. So during one of my seminars, I asked how many people had heard of keeping a priority list of things to do? Virtually everyone had. Then I asked how many people conscientiously made up a list of things to do every day, arranged the items in priority order, and crossed off each task as it was completed? I discovered that few people keep a list of things to do every day, although most people occasionally make a *To*

Do list when they are particularly busy, have a lot of things they want to remember to do, or have some particularly tight deadline." Lakein concludes his passage with a strong admonition that "only a daily list will do."[4]

A daily list provides the vehicle for you to consciously schedule time for projects that are important but not urgent. Only a well-prioritized *To Do* list will keep these productive activities in the open where you can remember to accomplish them.

MY EARLY TIME MANAGEMENT

There wasn't much emphasis on time management during those early days of our Christian organizations. The phrase hadn't yet been coined. My first awareness of the formal concept came in the early '60s when I began working with Alec Mackenzie on our joint book entitled, *Managing Your Time.*[5]

But despite the fact that I didn't write about the topic until 1967, I was always conscious of the value of time from the earliest days of my work experience.

In high school, I ran a print shop in my own basement. It seems like the first thing I needed to print was extra calendars to give me more time. Those long evening hours were very important in teaching me how to manage my time. I always kept a schedule to help me plan how much time I could spend in studies, running my shop and keeping up with other duties. In College, I ran the campus print shop plus my own printing plant. I was a college cook. I did my studies, and I was in sports. My wife remembers how I would cut our dates short because there were other things I wanted to do. While she didn't always appreciate my extra-curricular activities, those habits have kept me active and productive throughout my career.

THE GREATEST TIME SAVERS

At a management seminar in Chicago, 25 Christian executives were asked to compile a list of their most valuable time-saving techniques. Here's what they recommended:

A committee of two—Avoid involving unnecessary persons in the decision-making process.

Correspondence—fast answers. Jot down responses on letters or memos. Make a copy for your files, then return the original.

Correspondence—handle only once. Don't put it back in the pile! Answer it or put it where it can be answered.

Correspondence—follow-up file. If you must wait for information before answering, mark for F/U file (i.e., one week). Secretary pulls it out of the file in one week and returns to you with information necessary for answer.

Ensure understanding when delegating. Extra time invested to ensure complete understanding ultimately pays big dividends in time saved!

Appointment handling. Time taken to develop a good system pays off well.

Delegate reading. Why not? Benefits others besides yourself. Also gives you a picture of other talents of your team, while enormously broadening your coverage of important materials.

Conference phone call with pre-arranged agenda. Can accomplish amazing results at a fraction of the cost in time and travel money with from three to perhaps six persons in as many cities on the same hookup.

Have secretary answer correspondence. Aim to delegate as much of the correspondence as possible. One organization aims for 75 to 80 percent of all correspondence by secretaries, who sign the boss's name or present the complete file and letter for signature.

Write short memos and letters. Conscious effort here can bring amazing results.

Wastebasketry. Master the "quick toss" technique!

Form letters. Where the personal touch is not essential.

Planning and organizing time. As these executives said, "A look ahead may be worth two behind!"

A good secretary. Worth their weight in gold! There are excellent seminars offered for executive secretaries.

Management training. Careful selection of an occasional seminar provides needed break, objective view, solutions others have found to same problems, current thinking in the profession of management.

Trained staff. All of the foregoing applies to staff. Set the example, expect them to follow, let them know your expectations, then follow-up.

This list could go on, endlessly perhaps. But the important thing is to pick one or two of the more relevant suggestions and *put them to use.* They proved themselves yesterday. They work today. And they are needed even more tomorrow.

WHY YOU NEED THESE SKILLS— A LOOK AHEAD

The suggestions we've covered so far can be of enormous help in your own personal goals and private life. But they are also needed by the leaders who will tackle the larger problems of the world at large. As you put these time-saving concepts into use, I encourage you to remember the larger family our "elder brother" takes time to serve.

In March 1986, the world passed a significant milestone never before achieved. Global population reached 5 billion! When we think that during Christ's human life the total population was an estimated 250 million, it's staggering to think that over 20 times that number of people now live on this planet.

But what about tomorrow?

It has been estimated by the year 2000 world population will reach at least 6 billion. Every day the planet adds 250,000 people in need of leadership. That's 1,750,000 each week, 7.5 million a month, 90 million a year. The poorer nations account for 92 percent of this increase.

The population of the African nations will increase more than 65 percent by the year 2000—from 513 million to 850 million. The continent of Africa is probably the most needy in terms of absolute poverty in proportion to its entire populace, and the challenges facing it are increasing each year, even though it may be 50 percent Christian by the turn of the century.

Asian populace will increase 30 percent by the year 2000. That's an increase from 2.7 billion to nearly 3.6 billion, almost 900 million sheep without a shepherd in less than 15 years.

At the start of the twenty-first century, Mexico City will be the world's largest city with 28 million people; Shanghai next with 26 million; then Tokyo-Yokohama with 24 million; Peking, 23 million; Sao Paulo, 22 million; New York City, 20 million; Bombay, Calcutta, Jakarta and Rio de Janeiro will each have between 14-16 million souls.

There are no easy answers to the problem of world population growth. Economic and security concerns cause many of the world's parents to think they must have a sufficient number of children.

As our Lord looks at these expanding multitudes, He continues to have compassion on them, because they are harassed, and helpless—they are sheep without a shepherd. His words are still binding on us as present-day disciples: "The harvest truly *is* plentiful, but the laborers *are* few. Therefore pray the Lord of the harvest to send out laborers into His harvest" (Matt. 9:37,38).

THREE ARENAS

This mandate to be of service spotlights three major arenas of world need in which the enhancement of leadership and goal setting is essential. These include: (1) Those in need of spiritual bread, (2) those in need of physical bread and (3) those who are willing to prepare one or both of these meals.

The First Arena—Massive Gains, Massive Losses

The unprecedented spread of the gospel alongside the challenge of large groups of unreached peoples, or those in need of spiritual bread, make up the first arena.

My friend, Dr. David Barrett, noted author of the *World Christian Encyclopedia*, states the overall situation of Christianity is a picture of "massive gains offset by massive losses." In the Two-Thirds World, Christianity has undergone massive gains throughout the twentieth century. Most of us have heard of the dramatic growth of the church in China. Estimates range from 30-50 million believers—compared to 3 million at the beginning of the Revolution in 1949-50. Barrett estimates that in the continent of Africa, there are 6 million new Christians a year. Brazil, Argentina, Guatemala and the Philippines, among many other nations, also are experiencing unprecedented numbers of people declaring their newfound faith in Jesus Christ.

One of the greatest challenges facing Christianity now and in the twenty-first century is whether Christians will demonstrate to the poor, in deed, what they profess in words concerning love for their neighbor.

On the other hand, Christianity has shown massive losses in the Western and Communist worlds over the last 60 years. Europe and North America, for example, are losing nearly 2 million Christians a year, i.e., people who formerly called themselves by that name. In addition, in those parts of the world in which Islam, Hinduism or Buddhism are practiced, Christian conversion is considered a cultural invasion destructive to the society. We face the tremendous challenge of large groups of people who have extremely limited, if any, opportunity to become disciples of Jesus Christ.

The Second Arena—One Billion in Need

The second arena of leadership opportunity surrounds nearly 1 billion people in our world who now live in absolute poverty.

These "thousand million" human beings live with malnutrition, illiteracy and disease that go beyond any reasonable standard of decency. In addition, there are another 1 billion who eke out a living of under $235 per capita. The dual tragedy is that not only are these 2 billion people desperately poor, but nearly all of them are unevangelized. These groups represent over 40 percent of the world's population!

The need for leadership is overwhelming. One of the greatest challenges facing Christianity now and in the twenty-first century is whether Christians will demonstrate to the poor, in deed, what they profess in words concerning love for their neighbor. A great opportunity is before us to develop a new kind of Christian worker who will operate among the poor with skills to facilitate their healthy self-sufficiency, and with a heart desirous of introducing them to a new life in Jesus Christ.

Yet all of these regions are plagued by "brain-drain." John Perkins, board member for World Vision USA and founder of a ministry to rural blacks in the poorest state in America, found this to be true in his ministry. He states:

"The Black community in Mendenhall, Mississippi had few real leaders, few people with the vision and the skills to make a difference . . . Our best hope was to develop new leaders from among the young. The most promising, though, went off to college and few came back. They were the kind of highly motivated kids the big corporations wanted to hire. So why should they come back? What was there to come back to?"[7]

This question will have to be answered by leaders in the decades ahead.

The Third Arena—Salt, Light and Leaven

The third arena for leadership is Christian leaders penetrating their societies by being salt, light and leaven. In other words, those who are willing to provide spiritual and physical bread.

Incarnational-living or practicing Kingdom values is

sometimes the way World Vision describes the quality of Christian life it seeks to encourage in other believers. What we desire is a more effective penetration of the application of the Great Commission and the Great Commandment by Christians into the societies of the world.

There is a passage of Scripture that describes how one Christian leader can serve the needs of other leaders. God commanded Moses to, "Charge Joshua, and encourage and strengthen him; for he shall go over at the head of this people" (Deuteronomy 3:28, *RSV*).

In an attitude of humble service, each of us can help create opportunities for other Christian leaders to become: challenged to be more effective spiritual shepherds of the great hosts entering the Kingdom of God today and to reach out to those who have yet to respond positively to Jesus Christ; challenged to be involved in holistic development and to fill the leadership vacuum in needy communities; and challenged to penetrate their societies by being salt, light and leaven.

Encouraged when they are spiritually, emotionally and physically drained and exhausted.

Strengthened and supported in their struggles involving spiritual warfare, being change-agents in their communities and serving the people to whom God has called them.

Herbert Kane provides useful insight about the role of the missionary in the underdeveloped world in his book, *Understanding Christian Missions*. "Wherever missionaries have gone the story has been the same. They have consistently followed in the steps of their Master, who 'went about doing good' (Acts 10:38). In good times and bad they could always be depended on to be in the right place at the right time, healing, helping, serving, saving."[8]

Yet the act of doing good is not without its dilemmas

and riddles. Numerous questions arise and continue to grow in complexity for the leaders of the next century about the development of ministries.

Is it valid for a Christian agency to minister to individuals or communities only and leave untouched a political structure that oppresses people? The sordid details leaking out of Ethopia seem to confirm our worst suspicions. Yes, the appalling disaster of crop failures could have been avoided. And yes, certain government extremists used famine relief to remove and decimate their enemies. But can we refuse to help thousands because hundreds are mistreating millions? The questions multiply.

Do we have to convert the needy with whom we work, from, for example, Muslim to Christian to continue doing community development in a particular village?

What is good and bad development? We can never be sure of the eventual result. No one can predict the future. What looks promising now may wither; what seems marginal now may prosper.

How can the Western world feel it has developed enough to be able to tell the Two-Thirds World how to develop?

How does the difference between what we believe and how we live affect those we need to serve? Claiming the gospel is for the poor, many come to lesser developed countries with all the baggage of citizens of wealthy nations. Yet without the tools that have prospered our society, how could we have made any contribution at all?

Many of our leaders are called to work in countries where the political system is repressive. How can they speak out truthfully and still minister?

And finally, there is the paradox of the Apocalypse and the millennium. We are attempting to make the world better for mankind even as we proclaim the biblical prophecies that warn how things will become progressively worse till the Second Advent.

There are no simple answers for these dilemmas. But I do take consolation in the words of Herbert Kane's book about the vision of those who went before us. "It should be understood that in all their humanitarian endeavors the missionaries never lost sight of their primary goal, the evangelization of the non-Christian world. They would share the benefits of Western civilization, but not without the blessing of the gospel."[9]

These are the issues that plead for well-trained leaders who know how to set goals and plan their time. Imagine how much more fulfilling your personal accomplishments could be if you were also planning time to devote a part of your leadership energies to these wider wants!

IN SUMMARY

1. *Beware of how you spend your time.* You can't earn it back.

2. *Set meaningful goals.* If you don't know where you're going, you'll probably end up someplace else. And even if you do know where you're going, does your crew share your vision?

3. *Plan to plan.* If you fail to plan, you're planning to fail. The only difference is, you may be the last one to know.

4. *Make much ado about to do.* Charles Schwab paid $25,000 for this suggestion about the "to do list." How much is it worth to you?

5. *Use the great time savers of others.* Sixteen proven principles from 25 Christian executives.

6. *Prepare yourself to lead in the "Three Arenas."* This world of exploding population needs all the help it can get

from dedicated leaders who understand how to set and reach their goals.

With this knowledge of goal setting and time management, you can face the leadership challenges of tomorrow with greater confidence. But not complete confidence. Because more clues are needed for truly successful leadership as we shall see in chapter 3.

Chapter Three

MOTIVATION
Helping the
Performers Perform

*A person who has
helped develop a policy
will be less likely to
criticize it, more likely to
support it and generally
more eager to see it
implemented successfully.*

> *"I will act as if*
> *what I do makes a difference."*
> William James[1]

We live in an age of instant gratification. There's instant coffee warmed in the microwave, 56 channels on cable TV with instant access switching, instant replays and instant re-dialing telephones. Many of these instant features have been created by and for the new generation of American consumers who want the best and want it now.

The leadership principles we have discussed so far don't come instantly. They take hard work and time. But I am confident the same energy that has delivered our upscale society of the '80s can deliver the leadership required to guide this same society into the '90s and beyond. All that's required is the right kind of motivation.

After watching today's generation I'm convinced there's no such thing as an unmotivated person. Just watch a few people at break time, noon or closing time. The same ones who complain of heavy work loads, new procedures or pressures on the job will often race out the door to lift weights at the gym, or shop for new appliances.

People are motivated to do those things they feel are important, and often unresponsive toward things you feel are important. Something has to convince them that doing what you *want* will satisfy what they *need.*

In the previous chapters, we talked about the importance of commitment, goal setting and time management. However, these vehicles will go nowhere unless you continually refuel them with motivation. And it's not enough to fill your tank alone. You also need to replenish the motivation reservoir of everyone else on the team.

In the early days of my leadership training, we didn't understand the finer points of motivation. We simply kept on trying until we got results. But how many potential believers did we fail to convince for lack of the knowledge you're reading right now? With your motivation and your familiarity with instant results, imagine how much faster this knowledge can work for you.

In my earlier days I wanted to make a difference. That was one of my passions. The world was crying for direction and I was carrying a torch. It only made sense to stand up and run with it.

But I soon learned I could accomplish even more by helping the other runners advance. Earlier in my career I did not consider myself a particularly strong speaker or preacher, so I began looking for other ways to serve. Soon it became apparent I was an effective coordinator and platform manager. We all had a message we wanted to share, but somebody had to get the best music, best speakers, the best testimonies and put them together into an effective package.

I have always helped the performers to perform, and the motivators to motivate. And when you think about it, what skill better characterizes a leader? If you can't motivate others to follow, you're not leading, you're simply wandering around.

American entrepreneur John D. Rockefeller said, "I will pay more for the ability to deal with people than any other ability under the sun."

According to a report by the American Management Association, an overwhelming majority of the 200 managers who participated in a survey agreed that the most important single skill of an executive is the ability to get along with people. In the survey, management rated this ability more vital than intelligence, decisiveness, knowledge, or job skills.[2]

A HISTORY OF MOTIVATION

In the 1950s the evangelical community was rediscovering a challenge from half a century earlier. In the early 1900s, John R. Mott kindled an evangelical movement that blazed across several continents. "Let's evangelize the world in our generation," was the battle cry. Though others may have done so before them—who but God can judge the depth of Christian penetration at any one time—this band of dedicated believers was determined to "go ye therefore into all the world." We reasoned if it was needful for them in a simpler age and a smaller population, it was urgent for us at that time (1950). How much more so today?

Back then we were quick to help each other. It was nothing to pick up the phone and say, "Look, how would you handle this situation?" There was a network. Networking is a relatively new word, but it's not a new concept. Back then we had an entire network of evangelists who constantly motivated each other on the phone and in conferences.

I remember the first Youth for Christ conference I

ever attended. It was in 1946 at Medicine Lake, Minnesota. Fifty or 60 Christian leaders gathered together. I was tremendously impressed with the quality of those people and how they shared their experiences and encouraged each other. It was like a football team getting ready to go out on the field. Each personal ministry became part of the whole.

We believed the entire nation was being motivated by this group of young leaders. Here was the birth of many of today's para-church organizations. You never saw full-time youth leaders in the Church until organizations like Youth for Christ, Young Life and the Navigators came along and began to train these people. Now churches of any size have youth directors.

The lay ministry, such as Christian Business Men's Committee, and the Full Gospel Business Men's Association, all came out of that post-war era. Responsible civic leaders began to understand the effectiveness of their Christian witness and banded together. This was a whole new concept in motion. Pastors, evangelists and members of the apostolate enacted the principles of Ephesians 4 in dramatic fashion. Congregations began to equip the saints and the laity for the work of the ministry. That kind of teaching was new then.

Even Christian sports groups took root at that time. Today's Fellowship of Christian Athletes and Sports Ambassadors are by-products of that whole genre of the '40s and '50s. All because they were motivated.

WHAT IS MOTIVATION?

We've talked a great deal about the beneficial effects of motivation on Christian goals. But what is motivation? And how do you make it work?

Here's a definition I appreciate. It's simple, yet profound:

> Motivation is the act of creating circumstances
> that get things done through other people.

For years the most effective motivation in industry was assumed to be the use of arbitrary authority and the threat of its use to withhold benefits or to impose penalties. Time and motion studies became the vogue for maximizing working efficiency. Then came the realization that machinery and processes would run no better than people wanted them to. Slowdowns, strikes, apathy and disinterest could not be controlled with time and motion studies.

A person who has helped develop a policy will be less likely to criticize it, more likely to support it, and generally more eager to see it implemented successfully.

Studies conducted at the Hawthorne Works of Western Electric Company showed that simply putting a worker in a test situation provided sufficient interest and stimulation to ensure increased productivity even in the face of increasingly disadvantageous working conditions. Understanding what gives people a feeling of recognition and importance is of primary importance to the manager. People who sense in their leader the ability to help them satisfy their needs will follow willingly and enthusiastically.

Participation in the decision-making process has been identified as a strong factor in motivation and performance. A person who has helped develop a policy will be less likely to criticize it, more likely to support it, and generally more eager to see it implemented successfully.

The value of communication in developing motivation has often been overlooked. "Motivation to accomplish results," says Louis Allen, "tends to increase as people are informed about matters affecting these results."[3]

Principles of Human Behavior

Among the most important principles of human behavior of interest to managers are:

1. Behavior depends on both the person and the environment.
2. Each individual behaves in ways that make sense to to that individual.
3. An individual's perception of a situation influences personal behavior in that situation.
4. An individual's view of the self influences action.
5. An individual's behavior is influenced by needs, which vary from person to person and from time to time.

In other words you can motivate someone by changing the person, the situation or the person's feelings about the situation.

MOTIVATION IN ACTION

Robert Schuller tells the story of a friend who teaches physics and astronomy at Fullerton College. Many years ago this man began listening to Dr. Schuller's messages on positive thinking and self-esteem psychology. As he heard the principle on faith and positive programming, he wondered, "Will this work in my college classroom?"

Every year at that time 50 percent of the students who took the Introduction to Physics for science majors at Fullerton flunked. Consequently, every year in his first lecture the instructor would say, "I want to be honest with you. This is probably the toughest course you'll ever take. Fifty percent of you will flunk. It happens every year." He was right. Fifty percent of them always flunked.

However, after listening to the messages by Dr. Schuller, he decided to try a most audacious experiment. He stood before his incoming class and said, "Students, I have to tell you something. This introductory course in physics is very difficult. In fact, 50 percent of the students have failed this course every year. But I've been checking your records and I'm impressed with you. I am amazed at what an unbelievable class this is. You are all tremendously bright. In fact, I predict that for the first time in the history of this school, all of you will pass. None of you will flunk."

Later he confessed to Dr. Schuller that it was terribly frightening to make such a claim. However, he reported in a paper the following results: "I did not change my testing procedures one bit. And that year, every student in that class passed. Not one failed. I know I worked harder as a teacher, and the students did also."[4]

Understanding human behavior gets results. We've examined five principles of behavior. Our next step is to translate this understanding into a motivation checklist. But before explaining how to understand and influence others, let's make sure you understand yourself and your own influence as a leader. Here is a summary of the five main leadership styles. There's no right or wrong style. What works at one time will be ineffective another. What gets results by itself with one group will need to be combined with another style for a different group. It is important to remember that: (1) different leadership styles exist, and (2) different circumstances require different styles.

FIVE STYLES OF LEADERSHIP

1. *Laissez-faire*: No structure or supervision given; members set own goals and standards of performance; leader is "first among equals," without authority, a resource person.

2. *Democratic-participative*: Provides some structure and framework within which members still largely set own goals and standards; leader is an advisor with minimum authority.

3. *Manipulative-inspirational*: Some structure, usually confused and ambiguous; goals set by management with little participation, but employees' acceptance sought by "hard-sell."

4. *Benevolent-autocratic*: Activities or group largely structured; relatively close supervision; however, employees encouraged to make suggestions concerning their goals, working conditions, etc.

5. *Autocratic-bureaucratic*: Activities of group totally arbitrarily structured; participation by group in any context totally discouraged; supervision is authoritarian and autocratic; questioning of orders regarded as insubordinate.

HOW TO DRIVE PEOPLE WITHOUT DRIVING THEM OFF

Understanding the different styles of leadership we can better appreciate what a leader must do to motivate others.

Here is a checklist of 13 motivational levers, designed

to help you encourage others to take interest in what's important to you as a leader.

1. *Communicate standards and be consistent.* When a person knows that evaluation is according to a single, fair standard, that follower has a target to shoot for what isn't moving.

2. *Be aware of your own biases and prejudices.* No one is without biases. The question is whether or not you are aware of yours. (This would also include a knowledge of your biases for or against a given leadership style). How can you become more aware of your biases? One way is to keep a record of your prejudices. Check to see if your pre-judgments are accurate. If not, then change your attitude about that person. Invariably, emotional reactions color what should be effective, objective judgments. Be aware of yours.

3. *Let people know where they stand.* Carry out regular performance reviews. The positive or negative thoughts you have rattling about in your head serve no useful pur-pose to your people if you never tell them. Give each per-son sufficient attention. Let each man or woman, boy or girl, know you are looking for ways in which they can bet-ter themselves. Your honesty—spoken in positive, self-esteem enhancing ways—will create an atmosphere of trust. Without that trust, you could end up being the only passenger on your ship.

4. *Give praise when it is appropriate.* Properly handled, praise is one of the best motivation factors available to you as a leader. Avoid giving praise for every little thing done, because this will make your statements meaningless. Like any good seasoning, a little praise enhances a large serv-ing.

5. *Keep people informed of changes that may affect them.* If you plan to move your warehouse within a year, don't

wait until the moving vans arrive to tell your people. You don't have to divulge every company secret, but it's evidence of your concern if you keep your employees appropriately informed.

6. *Care about your employees.* If you have a suggestion box in the coffee room, or if you ask for comments from your church members, children or students, then by all means read those suggestions and listen to the comments. If you don't, they'll know it's no more than an idle exercise in your attempt to pretend you're interested.

7. *See people as ends, not means.* The conductor of an orchestra regards the musicians as individuals, but what kind of a concert would one big trumpet solo be? When the famous New World explorer James Cook discovered a new island, he named the discovery after the first man who spotted it. He regarded every man in his crew, even the ship's boy, as a partner in the adventure. If you are to succeed as a leader, Cook's example is a good discovery to remember.

8. *Build independence.* This is closely tied to caring for the people with whom you work. And yet, it is often a most frightening approach for a manager to take. If followers feel overly independent, they fear they will lose control. Actually, quite the opposite will occur. If you encourage a good worker to become independent, this person will become more loyal to you and to your organization. But try to keep a good person in a box and see what happens.

9. *Exhibit personal diligence.* There has never been a successful supervisor or executive—who could motivate others, who did not exhibit the qualities of self-motivation and commitment. We motivate by example. Believe it or not, employees actually like to feel as though they are living up to the image of their boss, especially if the boss is

devoted to the job of making the enterprise a smashing success. The people around you want to be a part of the success you are creating. And that's worth remembering.

10. *Be willing to learn from others.* Be honest with yourself. You don't know it all, no matter how smart you are. There's always someone some place who knows more about something than you do. Not to admit this could limit your potential for production and certainly reduce your impact on the marketplace or society. The old adage remains true: You can do just about anything you want if you don't care who gets the credit.

11. *Demonstrate confidence.* Show by your behavior and language that you are confident of your own abilities—and that you share that same confidence with those who work or live with you. As Scripture puts it, "Good men long to help each other" (Prov. 12:12 *TLB*). There is nothing that builds esprit de corps within the family, the church, the business, the ministry or the community more than expressions of mutual confidence. Once we indicate that we believe in the other person's integrity, motivation and personhood, we form a bond as strong as a cable strung together from individual pieces of wire.

12. *Delegate, delegate, delegate.* We'll have more to say on this important principle in chapter 7 on decision making. The leader who creates, delegates and moves on to still more creative activity, will soon wind up leading the pack. But woe to the leader who must know every detail, every purchase order and the daily schedule of every employee. The inability to delegate has been proven again and again to be the most common reason for leadership failure. Are you willing to turn loose some of your responsibility? If so, you'll find you're really not giving it away at all. You're cultivating its growth.

13. *Encourage ingenuity.* This technique works with

everyone. Even the lowest paid clerk can be creative. Challenge the people who work or live with you to "beat your system." If, for example, your filing system leaves something to be desired, don't you change it. Have others recommend the changes. You'll be surprised at the wealth of ideas generated. Start a list. And as you begin to think of and develop it, you will find that such a list is endless. Go to it!

MOTIVATED BY THINGS ON EARTH

If you have difficulty motivating people for "things above," it is often helpful to stand back and survey what is motivating them here below.

Recently Consumers Union published a book that reviewed "50 small wonders and big deals" of the past half century. It listed those things that motivated most Americans in the past 50 years. *Newsweek* magazine followed up with its own list of the top 10 "things" on the consumer hit parade. The following inventions help explain why we do the things we do.

Consumer Hit Parade—The Top 10

1. *Television.* We don't even agree on its full effects. Does it promote violence? TV has surely changed politics; it brought the Vietnam War into our living rooms. It's also expanded national culture, from sitcoms to pro football. In 1945 there were only 8,000 television sets; by 1960 nearly 90 percent of our homes had one.

2. *Jet Travel.* It has shrunk the country. The year 1985's 380 million passengers were nearly 7 times greater than the number in 1960 and 54 times more than in 1945. Jets, which began service in 1958, made both planes and

crews far more productive. Adjusted for inflation, air fares have dropped two-thirds since 1945.

3. *The Pill.* Introduced in 1960, the Pill—along with working women and better appliances—subverted old sex roles. There was more sex and fewer babies; the birthrate turned down in the 1960s. Fears of adverse side effects now rank the Pill behind sterilization (used mostly by married women) as a contraceptive.

4. *Air Conditioning.* It made the sun belt possible. Before the war air conditioners were rare in offices and almost nonexistent in homes. The 1960s were the first decade since the Civil War that the South experienced more in-migration than out-migration.

5. *Automatic Washers and Dryers.* They revolutionized housework. In 1940 dryers barely existed, and only a minority of homes had cumbersome wringer-washers. Hand laundering was sheer drudgery—"a moving stairway to the grave," said Edison. More than two-thirds of households now have washers and dryers.

6. *Antibiotics.* Before antibiotics, as Consumer Union reports, even the "cuts of everyday living could be life-threatening." Penicillin suppressed infections but wasn't used until World War II. After the war other antibiotics proliferated.

The things we value reveal the ideas we cherish.

---

7. *Health Insurance.* It has made health care an entitlement—something due everyone—and promoted growth of doctors and hospitals. In 1940 patients paid four-fifths of medical costs directly. Now government and

private insurance pay nearly three-quarters.

8. *Long Distance.* It too has shrunk America. In 1945, 54 percent of homes didn't have a phone. Long-distance direct dialing didn't begin until 1951, and operators handled most calls until the 1960s. Better technology has cut rates (after inflation) by more than 85 percent since 1940; calling volumes are more than 30 times higher.

9. *Social Security and Pensions.* Retirement is now an expected part of life—something not true before the war. As late as 1948 nearly half the men over 65 worked. Social security, enacted in 1935, was vastly expanded after the war.

10. *Interstate Highways.* They've shaped suburbia by attracting offices, malls and industrial parks, determining where we live, work and shop. The interstates, 1 percent of our roads, carry a fifth of the traffic.[5]

Newsweek left computers out of the list because they mainly serve business and not the individual. But this gives you a quick snapshot of what motivates the average American. The things we value reveal the ideas we cherish. I see a lot of comfort and convenience here—which is not necessarily wrong—as long as they're included in the service of Christ.

EQUAL RIGHT, EQUAL PRIDE

So far we've seen a lot of principles and examples. Here's a story that helps tie them all together by illustrating motivation in action.

During the Second World War, Winston Churchill, a man respected and admired, was going up and down his scarred country trying to marshal the moral will of the people to withstand the assault of the enemy. He visited troops and factories and then someone suggested that he call on the coal miners. "If you could just stop in one of the little coal-mining towns, Mr. Churchill," one man pleaded. "They don't get their pictures in the paper and they never receive any credit."

So Winston Churchill went down to visit the hardworking coal miners. He gazed at the greasy faces of these tough miners as they gathered—shocked that Winston Churchill would come to talk to them! And the words he spoke that October day will never be forgotten. Standing before them he said:

> "We will be victorious! We will preserve our freedom. And years from now when our freedom is secure and peace reigns, your children and your children's children will come and they will say to you, 'What did you do to win our freedom in that great war?' And one will say, 'I marched with the Eighth Army!' Someone else will proudly say, 'I manned a submarine.' And another will say, 'I guided the ships that moved the troops and the supplies.' And still another will say, 'I doctored the wounds!'"

Then he paused. The dirty-faced miners, with their caps pushed back, sat in silence and awe waiting for him to continue.

> "They will come to you," he shouted, and you will say, with equal right and equal pride, 'I cut the coal! I cut the coal that fueled the ships that moved the supplies! That's what I did. I cut the coal.'"[6]

Now that's motivation! But it still doesn't compare with the greatest motivator of all time.

THE GREATEST MOTIVATOR

The person who epitomizes these traits of motivation is none other than Jesus Christ.

He was conceived by the Father of all humanity to encourage people of every age to join His family.

He was the Son of God, but He enjoyed conducting His work through fishermen, tax collectors, homemakers and other repentant sinners.

He grew up as a humble carpenter, but He motivated His believers to construct an everlasting, spiritual temple.

He possessed the power to call legions of angels from heaven, but He allowed the prince of darkness to slay Him in lieu of His followers who actually deserved the punishment.

He spoke with authority, but He listened with compassion. He was tough, but gentle. Not the poet's "pale Galilean," Jesus Christ was motivation incarnate. As a member of the God family, He could have accomplished everything He needed to do toward us sinful humans with impersonal clouds, pillars of fire, thunder and miracles. But instead, He chose to meet us at eye level as a fellow human being and give you and me the opportunity to follow His lead and motivate our loved ones to do the same.

There is no greater opportunity nor challenge than to walk as He walked and motivate as He motivated.

IN A NUTSHELL

1. *Look to the accomplishments of those in the past as a source of ideas and motivation for the future.* Innovations such as Youth for Christ and The Full Gospel Businessmen's Association can trigger new ideas.

2. *Remember the five principles of human behavior.*

These will help you create the circumstances that get things done through other people.

3. *Pick the best leadership style* or combination of styles. There are five to choose from.

4. *Review the 13 motivational levers.* If you want to move others, you have to know the right switch.

5. *Be aware of the distractions caused by the Consumer Hit Parade.* We are all motivated to seek food, shelter and clothing. But for some, this motivation borders on compulsion.

Our need to motivate and be motivated has never been greater. If I as an older leader and you as a young leader fail the calling, we join the ranks of those who regard their time on earth as nothing more than apprenticeship for death. If we succeed, then we're ready to add the next dimension of leadership, one which supplies the secret ingredient for success, our topic in chapter 4.

Chapter Four

ENTHUSIASM
The Secret Ingredient
for Success

Things cannot remain
as they are. The world
sorely needs "change
agents" to affect a real
difference. And that takes
enthusiasm. We need to
make people restless.

> *"The only difference
> between a puddle and a geyser
> is enthusiasm."*
> Anonymous

We live in the age of high-speed information. But we're saddled with an organizational structure straight out of the Roman empire. This is a major dilemma in the Church. God inspired a system of elders and ministers ideally suited for the day of foot traffic, horse and sailing vessel. Today He relies upon our faith and ingenuity to make it work in a time of jet travel and satellite hook-ups.

This split has been a source of great frustration to many of today's young leaders. The very leaders who possess the imagination and enthusiasm to overcome these problems are all too often turned off by the necessity. Now more than ever before, our Church needs the optimism, energy and entrepreneurship of today's young thinker, who is almost always enthusiastic. And much enthusiasm is needed in the work of the Lord!

Enthusiasm—"Infused with god." What could better explain this word that derives its meaning from the Greek roots *EN*, meaning "in" and *THEOS*, "god"? We all recognize enthusiasm when we see it. But how does it work? And why? These answers often remain a secret. The dictionary uses lower case *g* in spelling the word *god*. Al Capone was enthusiastic. But there was certainly nothing capital about the god infusing him.

How can you and I become infused with the true God in a manner that will propel us toward lasting success? Let's examine this important ingredient along with a recipe for using it effectively.

SKY HIGH ENTHUSIASM

I remember traveling aboard a DC-4 in 1953 to an evangelism conference in Ireland. Engine problems grounded us in Gander, Newfoundland for 24 hours. But did our group sit around waiting and relaxing? No! In that 24 hours we organized a public meeting in the airport for hundreds of people. The Palermo Brothers were singing and several of us preached and testified. We probably had three hours of meetings right there in the airport, and the people were entranced by this group of young men and women who were sharing their faith in Jesus Christ.

Then a radio station came out and taped some of the things we were doing. The next day as we were flying out of Gander, the pilot came on the intercom and said, "I have something I want you folks to hear." And he turned on the Gander radio station. There was the service we had the night before outrunning us through the airwaves as we headed toward Ireland for the next "infusion."

Amazing! These enthusiasts never missed an opportunity. They weren't going to just sit around the lobby; they wanted to have a meeting. They wanted to share, to testify. They were filled with "theos" and wanted nothing more than to share it with others. The more enthusiasm they gave away, the more we all possessed.

That reminds me of another airborne incident in 1958 on our way back from Sao Paulo, Brazil. Everyone was so excited about the miracles God had performed at our Congress that we all got together in the back of the chartered DC-4. Spontaneously, we started singing, rejoicing, testifying and celebrating the eminently successful campaign. Soon the captain sent word back saying, "The ship is out of balance. You'll have to return to your seats." Apparently, that which lifts your spirits doesn't always do the same for an aircraft. But it's times like these that help you feel the influx of something more real than the physical.

FORGET THE 95 MILLION IF YOU CAN'T EVANGELIZE SIXTY

One evangelist discovered that Christians have a lot to learn about enthusiasm for taking the gospel to secularized people. Here are some telling excerpts from Jim Petersen's book *Evangelism As a Life-style.*

"In 1963 my family traveled by ship from the United States to Brazil. There were 120 people on board. Half were tourists and half were missionaries—including us. Sixty missionaries and sixty tourists! A one-to-one ratio for sixteen days. Since there isn't much more to do aboard ship other than walk, read, or converse, I couldn't imagine how any of those tourists could get through the trip without receiving a thorough exposure to the Christian message. More ideal conditions for evangelism couldn't exist.

"During the first three days my wife and I spent our time relating to the other passengers. Conversations were unhurried and soon we found ourselves deeply involved in discussing Christ with our new acquaintances.

"On the third day I thought that if the other fifty-eight

missionaries were doing what we were, we would have a serious case of overkill. I decided to check with the others about coordinating our efforts. My first opportunity came when I encountered six missionaries sitting together on the deck. I joined them and expressed my concern that we get our signals straight so we wouldn't overwhelm the passengers.

"I had totally misjudged the problem. When I explained what was on my mind, the six just looked at one another. Apparently, it hadn't occurred to them to talk to the other sixty passengers about Christ. Finally one said, 'We just graduated from seminary and didn't learn how to do that sort of thing there.' Another said, 'I don't know. I have sort of a built-in reservation against the idea of conversion.' A third said, 'I've been pastor for three years, but I've never personally evangelized anyone. I don't think I know how either.'

"I remember saying that if we, in sixteen days and with a one-to-one ratio, couldn't evangelize sixty people, we might as well forget about ninety-five million Brazilians. Perhaps it would be just as well if we would all catch the next boat north."

Enthusiasm is contagious. Once infected you can pass it along to others with ease and joy.

What was missing? Jim Petersen's book recounts how he motivated the other "evangelists" to begin fulfilling their purpose by sharing the spirit that burned within him.[1]

Thus we discern several valuable lessons about enthusiasm. Like a childhood disease, you get it from somebody who had it before. Classes, books, buildings and job titles won't automatically infuse you with God—unless they drive you into contact with a real live "carrier." We also discover that enthusiasm is contagious. Once infected you can pass it along to others with ease and joy.

SQUARE MEALS AT A ROUND TABLE

We've concentrated so far on enthusiasm for God and His Word. That, of course, is the primary thrust of this book. But sometimes it's easier to behave properly at a formal occasion when you've had enough practice at the casual events. Here are a few examples of enthusiasm in the secular world that illuminate important principles.

Enthusiasm for Dollars

An associate of mine tells the story about his wife, who had lost a contact lens. She looked all around the bedroom for it. But the more she looked for it, the more frustrated she became. "Why do these things happen to me? Here I am in a hurry and now I've lost a contact lens! Where is it?" Then she told her husband about the problem.

One of the first things he wanted to know was, "How much is it going to cost me to replace this thing?" Upon hearing the figure of $25, he went into the bedroom with a different spirit of enthusiasm. Within minutes he had located the missing lens.

"How come I looked all over for this thing and couldn't find it? Then you walk in and practically pick it right up. What's the difference?" asked the woman.

"Well, you were looking for a contact lens," he explained. "And I was looking for $25."

The power of enthusiasm!

Poor Eyesight, Rich Vision

"I had only one eye," she writes, "and it was so covered with dense scars that I had to do all my seeing through one small opening in the left of the eye. I could see a book only by holding it up close to my face and by straining my one eye as hard as I could to the left." And so begins an amazing story of enthusiasm and perseverance as recounted in the Dale Carnegie classic, *How to Stop Worrying and Start Living.*

Borghild Dahl was virtually blind for half a century. Yet she saw enough to behold the power of enthusiastic determination. She refused to be pitied, refused to be considered different. As a child, she wanted to play hopscotch with other children, but she couldn't see the markings. So after the other children had gone home, she got down on the ground and crawled along with her eye near to the marks. She memorized every bit of the ground where she and her friends played and soon became an expert at running games. She did her reading at home, holding a book of large print so close to her eye that her eyelashes brushed the pages. She went on to earn two college degrees: a B.A. from the University of Minnesota and an M.A. from Columbia University.

Borghild started teaching in the tiny village of Twin Valley, Minnesota, and rose until she became professor of journalism and literature at Augustana College in Sioux Falls, South Dakota. She taught there for 13 years, lecturing before women's clubs and giving radio talks about books and authors. "In the back of my mind," she writes, "there had always lurked a fear of total blindness. In order to overcome this, I had adopted a cheerful, almost hilarious, attitude toward life."

Then in 1943, when she was 52-years-old, a miracle

happened: an operation at the famous Mayo Clinic. She could now see 40 times better than she had ever been able to see before.

A new exciting world of loveliness opened before her. She now found it thrilling even to wash dishes in the kitchen sink. "I began to play with the white fluffy suds in the dishpan," she writes. "I dip my hands into them and I pick up a ball of tiny soap bubbles. I hold them up against the light, and in each of them I can see the brilliant colors of a miniature rainbow."

As she looked through the window above the kitchen sink, she saw "the flapping gray-black wings of the sparrows flying through the thick, falling snow."

She found such ecstasy looking at the soap bubbles and sparrows that she closed her book *I Wanted to See* with these words: "'Dear Lord,' I whisper, 'Our Father in heaven, I thank Thee. I thank Thee.'"

Dale Carnegie ended his chapter of this story with an obvious admonition. "Imagine thanking God because you can wash dishes and see rainbows in bubbles and sparrows flying through the snow. All the days of our years we have been living in a fairyland of beauty, but we have been too blind to see, too satiated to enjoy. If you want to stop worring and start living, count your blessings — not your troubles."[2]

RECIPE FOR SUCCESS

These accomplishments by Borghild Dahl demonstrate the power of our secret ingredient. But what's so secret about enthusiasm? Unlike the formula for Coca-Cola that's locked in a safe and known to only a handful of specialists, everyone sees and understands enthusiasm. But every good cook knows it's one thing to gather up ingredients and quite another to stir them together into a delicious, taste-tempting treat. As you examine our recipe for success, keep in mind that having a cookbook on the shelf doesn't put the meal on the table. You've got to stir up some action.

Recipe for Success

A. Gather these ingredients

1. A worthy goal

2. Facts, information, knowledge and experience

3. Good health and a positive outlook

4. Determination

5. Tenacity and perseverance

6. Ingenuity and creativity

7. Prayer

B. Now put them all together with:

ENTHUSIASM

The reason this last ingredient is secret is the simple fact that enthusiasm is not a separate ingredient of itself. Rather it is a companion of all the others.

We can't accomplish anything unless we attack it with enthusiasm. We can't be placid and settle for the status quo. That's unacceptable. It's not even biblical. Things cannot remain as they are. The world sorely needs "change agents" to affect a real difference. And that takes enthusiasm. You and I need to make people restless.

That's the purpose of preaching—to make people dissatisfied with where they are by helping them understand there's something better beyond. To the new generation of leaders coming along today I say: Come share some of your enthusiam for life with our joy for the afterlife.

ENTHUSIASM TRAINING

Is it possible to learn how to increase our enthusiasm through merely studying a book? I cannot guarantee that reading the pages of this book will infuse you with God and His power. But I can guarantee if you do those things that enthusiastic people do, you will benefit. And one thing enthusiastic people do is improve themselves through study and training in the fields that are important.

I believe the most successful leaders place personnel development among their highest priorities. Millions of dollars are spent each year in industry for management development and training programs. But still there appears to be a shortage of strong leadership potential. There may be two reasons for this.

One is that promotion is emphasized far more than development; the other is that development is frequently not supported at top management levels. Without realizing it, leaders often doom the ultimate success of programs because they show too little active interest, though they may give token consent or encouragement to their key people. These factors are equally damaging to the development of Christian leadership.

TRAINED WITH ENTHUSIASM

A few Christian leaders have the mistaken assumption they don't need to be trained. After all, they're led by God

Himself. What can mere mortals teach them? Consider that a number of people in the Bible were trained for leadership even though they had received a call from God. The best example is probably the disciples, who were trained at the feet of Jesus for three years. In His high priestly prayer to the Father before His death, Jesus alluded to those things He had passed on to the Twelve in order to perpetuate His work on earth. "For I have passed on to them the commands you gave me; and they accepted them and know of a certainty that I came down to earth from you, and they believe you sent me" (John 17:8, *TLB*).

A prophet of God in the Old Testament period was specifically called to enunciate His truths to the world. Yet under Samuel's direction an actual school—the school of the prophets—was set up to train these leaders (see 1 Sam. 19:18-20). It was here that David no doubt found refuge from Saul who at that time wanted to destroy him. During the time of Elijah and Elisha such training schools were located at Gilgal, Bethel and elsewhere (see 2 Kings 2:1-3; 4:38; 6:1). According to Jewish tradition, these schools trained students throughout the long history of Judah to fill the office of prophet. There were many of these seers or scribes, for the Old Testament frequently alludes to prophets in the plural.

Such schools were the forerunner of the Jewish rabbinic centers following the return of the captives from Babylon under the direction of Ezra, Nehemiah and Zerubbabel. The theological schools of the early church were a direct outgrowth of this concept, and the modern seminary is the extension in our time. (I only wish there were more than the 100,000 students enrolled in seminaries out of 12,000,000 American college students today.)

The purpose of the schools was always threefold: to develop, train and educate men in the leadership functions necessary to perpetuate God's work. We may safely conclude that spiritual gifts can be developed.

Other biblical references demonstrate the need and justification for developing gifts within people to place them in positions of leadership. Moses trained his successor Joshua. Joshua was discovered in the battle against the Amalekites; Moses saw his potential immediately and groomed him to become the undisputed leader of the people. Numbers 27:16 states that God would give His people direction through the appointment of a man. But the calling required training and supervision. For many years Moses shared his leadership responsibilities with Joshua.

Training was an important part of the formation of the early church and the work of the apostle Paul. Remember that the training of people was the key for the rapid expansion of the church in the first century. Paul trained Timothy, Barnabas, Silas and John Mark. He was also responsible for the growth of Sopater, Aristarchus, Secundus, Gaius, Tychicus, Trophimus and others whom he mentions in his Epistles.

Paul could have appealed simply to his special gift of apostleship and let it go at that, trying to do all the work himself. But he wisely followed the course of preparing others and helping to establish those with whom he shared the gospel.

Our missionary and evangelical enterprises are doomed today in the Third World if our leaders, both from the West and in the developing nations, do not develop leadership among Christian nationals. Thank God, this seems to be an increasing emphasis in these younger churches in the Third World. People like John Haggai and my World Vision Indian colleague, Dr. Sam Kamaleson, are making a tremendous impact in this ministry.

Dr. John Gardner makes a poignant observation in his

book, *Excellence*. "The society that scorns excellence in plumbing because plumbing is a humble activity, and tolerates shoddiness in philosophy because it is an exalted activity, will have neither good plumbing nor good philosophy. Neither its pipes nor its theories will hold water."[3]

I have known executives who approach golf, skiing or tennis with more intense effort than they approach their task as leaders. Excellence requires more than reading a book on management principles. Professional expertise demands that we take continual action for improvement. And that requires enthusiasm.

Such reluctance is due in part to a false perception of success. To succeed is to "sell out" in the eyes of many Christians. Yes, Christ warned us that we cannot serve God and mammon. But He never told us we cannot use mammon. In fact, He later admonished, "Make friends for yourselves by unrighteous mammon . . . Therefore if you have not been faithful in the unrighteous mammon, who will commit to your trust the true *riches*?" (Luke 16:9,11). I happen to agree with Hendrik van Loon when he says, "In history as in life, it is success that counts."[4] But our success must always be measured by God's yardstick.

Ordway Tead in his helpful book *The Art of Leadership* examines the various methods of giving expression to leadership training. He provides five methods of instruction that may be adapted to unlock enthusiasm in a potential leader.

Methods of Leadership Training

1. Experience in a leadership situation under some supervision
2. Progression from small to larger leadership situations

3. Apprentice courses of practice and study

4. Conference study of methods by groups of leaders

5. Systematic personal conferences of trainer and leader.[5]

Development is fundamental, and it has to be measured or quantified in some way. If potential leaders have not learned to use effectively the material being taught them, the training program must be revised. Several criteria can measure this factor, although admittedly it is not easy. Ordway Tead offers five suggestions that help quantify the impact of enthusiasm.

Evaluation of Leadership

1. The volume of work done by the group the individual leads. It may be possible to measure this in terms of volume or cost per unit of man hours.
2. The quality of work done by the group. Sometimes this can be done be inspection, sometimes by studies of attitudes of clients, (colleagues,) [sic] customers or the public.
3. The stability of membership in the group. If there is a marked tendency for people to enter the group and then quickly resign, that is a bad sign. Figures of "labor turnover" are used in many organizations to discover such a tendency. And figures of the number of individuals who have stayed with the group for a given number of years can further show how stable the group is.

4. The number of complaints or grievances that is brought to the responsible directors of the group.
5. The opinion of the members of the group as to their own state of mind in relation to dealings with the leaders. [6]

With this understanding of the relationship between leadership training and enthusiasm, here are several helpful steps suggested by my friend Frank Goble in his book *Excellence in Leadership*.

As An Enthusiastic Leader . . .

I will reserve the following dates and times for an improvement program.

I will schedule a meeting with my staff to plan an organizational improvement program. Who? When? Where?

I will start holding regular meetings with my staff as the first step toward adopting the coordinated team approach at all levels under my jurisdiction. Who? When? Where?

I will attend some seminars. Which seminars? When?

I will start reading leadership literature. What? When?

I will start a leadership library. How? When? Where?

I will obtain and display some signs to remind me and my associates to do things in a professional way.

I will analyze my own use of time. This is how I will proceed:

I will seek a qualified consultant to help improve personal and organizational effectiveness. Who? When?

The area which shows the greatest possibility for improvement is:

I will start there. What? How? When?

I will do the following:

This checklist is a tool to identify those areas needing improvement. The list can and should be expanded and adapted to your individual needs.[7]

THE UNITED WORLDS OF AMERICA

God has many jobs waiting for your enthusiastic leadership. These help us realize the importance of refining our personal skills and offering them to the Lord. In a keynote address to the National Convocation on Evangelizing Ethnic America, held in Houston, Texas in May 1985, C. Peter Wagner gave a startling interpolation of the 1980 census figures. His numbers show that American Anglos are now a minority group. The United States of America is less a melting pot and more of a potpourri of divergent cultures and ethnic groups.

Ethnic Worlds of America in 1980

	Millions	Percent
Europeans	94	41
Anglos	67	29
Blacks	26.5	11
Hispanics	23	10
Asians	3.5	1.5
American Indians	3.5	1.5
Totals	231.5	100

The implications of this reality are enormous. Since the Civil Rights movement of the 1960s, what was once thought to be a single nation has melted into one main course to become a group of many nationalities served up as a smorgasbord of ethnic interests.

Minorities now make up a majority in at least 25 major U.S. cities, including Miami, Newark, Washington, Atlanta, Detroit, El Paso, New Orleans, Chicago, Hartford and Jersey City, to name a few. Miami is the second largest Cuban city. Downtown stores carry window signs "English Spoken Here."

There are more Jews in New York City than in Tel Aviv. Chicago is the world's second largest Polish city, and

Los Angeles is the second largest Mexican city. There are more Hispanics in Los Angeles than in seven of the Latin American countries. The U.S. is the fifth largest Spanish-speaking country in the world. New York is the second largest Puerto Rican city. The projection is that by the year 2000, more than 50 major U.S. cities will be predominantly ethnic minority and California may revert to a Spanish-speaking state.

Why give special attention to these products of the new Ellis Islands? Jesus said, "Go therefore and make disciples of all the nations" (Matt. 28:19). The Greek from which "all nations" is translated is *panta ta ethne*. *Ethne*, of course, is the word from which our English word "ethnic" is derived. Because our Lord has commanded us to evangelize *panta ta ethne*, many American Christian leaders have been developing a new awareness of ethnic America.

One thing we know is that American ethnics are under-evangelized. While about 74 percent of America's 26.5 million blacks are affiliated with churches, and about 68 percent of whites are church members, this is not true for most of the other ethnic groups. Hispanics of the protestant *Evangelico* number less than 4 percent according to studies in Los Angeles. C. Peter Wagner projects similar figures for most ethnic groups across the nation. We know for sure that 3 million Muslims and 2.4 million Hindus are almost totally unevangelized. Earl Parvin, in his recently published book *Mission USA* estimates that 95 percent of Native Americans, Franco-Americans, and recent immigrants are unevangelized.[8]

Despite a veritable Babylon of confusion, much is being done to reach these peoples. Most of the ethnic minorities live in the cities and the Lausanne Strategy Working Group under the leadership of Ray Bakke has developed a high level urban program. Southern Baptists have set the pace with their Language Missions Division. Every Sunday more than 4,600 language-culture congregations worship in 87 languages.

Other denominations—significantly crossing ethnic barriers in the United States—include the Church of the Nazarene and the Assemblies of God. The textbook for the Houston '85 National Convocation for Evangelizing Ethnic America, *Heirs of the Same Promise,* mentions denominations such as the United Methodist Church, which has adopted "developing and strengthening the ethnic minority local church" as its missional priority through 1988.[9]

If we can't evangelize the ethnic groups in our own society, how can we successfully reach those in other lands?

The Lutheran Church of America is seeing considerable growth in black, Hispanic, Asian, and American Indian churches. The Presbyterian Church (U.S.A.) has 100 Native American congregations. Even the Christian Reformed Church, a traditionally Dutch denomination, now has churches worshiping in 11 different languages. If present trends continue, there will be more Asians than Dutch in their American congregations.

Here we discover entire worlds within one nation, all enthusiastic for their own language, culture, music, history, religion—their own identity. How much less enthusiastic can we be in spreading the truth about the God who created all men of one blood and one family? If we can't evangelize the ethnic groups in our own society, how can we successfully reach those in other lands?

ENTHUSIASM OVERVIEW

1. Look to the examples of yesterday for ways you can share your enthusiasm today.

2. Discover the enthusiastic joys of personal evangelism.

3. Let the personal triumphs of others inspire you to new heights of enthusiasm.

4. Cook up the Recipe for Success often—with bushels of enthusiasm.

5. Be willing to learn from others through formal and informal training.

6. Take positive steps for putting your enthusiasm into action for improvement at home, on the job and in the Church.

7. Look on the kaleidoscope of ethnic diversity in our land as a continual reminder of how much we need *enthusiastic* participation in service to the Lord.

I've characterized enthusiasm as the secret ingredient for success. It's secret only because it becomes, through second nature, an unnamed part of everything a successful leader thinks and does. We've seen the rules, the examples and the checklists for enthusiasm. All we need now is the determination and the willpower to put this information into action.

Borghild Dahl spent untold hours overcoming obstacles by examining things as close as an eyelash. Are you willing to open your healthy eyes to the soul saving truth in front of us here? Before you answer too quickly, please make sure you're handling the issues with heartfelt honesty—the topic of chapter 5.

Chapter Five

HONESTY
Say What You Mean
and Mean What You Say

Mr. Boesky thought he
could rewrite 50 years
of ethics about trading
on the stock market. He
wound up receiving the
largest fine ever imposed
by the Securities and
Exchange Commission.

> *"Some of the best fiction
> of our day can be found on the
> expense reports of Christian Organizations."*
> Anonymous

Many years ago a prominent radio preacher surprised me with his candor. We were neighbors and he came over for coffee one evening. "You know, Ted, this is terrible to confess, but I really don't like people."

I said, "Well, how in the world can you be a pastor?"

"That's why I'm not a good pastor," he said. "That's why I need to get back into radio."

I always admired his honesty.

How many people have the honesty to admit they're not good at what they're doing and need to make a change? We tend to think of honesty as little more than obedience to the commandment, "Thou shalt not steal" (Exod. 20:15, *KJV*). But as we explore this subject we discover there's a great deal more to honesty than physical objects in need of protection.

First, however, we cannot escape the mammon of unrighteousness. A successful congregation, blessed by

God, is going to generate a substantial amount of income. When you're responsible for that much money, it's easy to get careless with the accounting and stewardship. A personal payment here, a questionable trip there. Before long you're mingling God's money with yours like paper clips and rubber bands in a junk drawer.

Many old-timers remember the love offering. This was a special collection taken up exclusively for the care of the preacher. The more dynamic and popular the minister— and the message—the more "salary" collected. Decades ago, Billy Graham pioneered in doing away with this temptation and instituted a regular salary for the evangelists. I applaud him highly.

In the late 1970s I had the privilege, and pain, of reviewing our national charitable giving practices. This experience led to the formation of a national council. The country had undergone a prominent scandal some years earlier involving the Pallottine Fathers. In 1975, two reporters for the *Baltimore Sun* discovered that the Pallottine order, mailing as many as 100 million letters a year in charity appeals, was funneling large sums into a variety of other operations—monetary and political. They collected millions of dollars, which donors thought were all going to the poor. This event—along with several other public disclosures—spurred many religious organizations into a closer examination of their financial dealings.

Over 150,000 inquiries a year poured into the Better Business Bureau concerning the honesty of charitable organizations.

In December 1977, several of us invited representatives of 32 evangelical Christian groups to meet in Chicago to decide on their response to mounting pressure for reform. Over the next few months, a steering committee developed standards that would be applicable to evangelical groups and sought to communicate with others who were not at the original sessions. In March 1979, the Evangelical Council for Financial Accountability (ECFA) was formed, grouping more than 1,100 evangelical organizations, with a total 1975 income of $1 billion from 25-30 million donors. It was my privilege to serve as chairman of the board of the ECFA for its first three years. There I learned, firsthand, the importance of total honesty in dealing with Christian monies.

Without a doubt these lessons from the past inform the future.

TRANSPARENT LIVES

This matter of honesty is more than dollars and cents; it's more than lying or cheating. What we really need is transparency in our lives. Certainly all of us, if we will admit it, are tempted to fudge on income tax reporting or other expense records. And what about the other temptations?

What happens in your hotel room when you can spend $5.25 to see a pornographic movie without getting caught? Is that being honest? There's the matter of playing footsie with the opposite sex. I know a brother who would say, "let me pray for you, sister—in my office"—and insist on wrapping "sister" in his arms as he prayed.

I had a dear friend who is now in heaven. He would sneak off after a meal to get a smoke. When nobody was watching him on an airplane, he would order his after dinner cocktail while traveling to deliver a message about the evils of sin and drink. Now this man was a strong Christian leader. But how many accomplishments of the spirit did he drive away with one clink of a glass?

We can easily condemn such obvious dishonesty. But what about our refined indiscretions? It's equally dishonest to preach on the value of a quiet time when you've never done it yourself. It's dishonest to talk about the power of prayer and lead a prayerless life. It's dishonest to talk about forgiveness and fail to forgive. In short, it's dishonest to practice sin and preach righteousness.

Solomon warned us about the little foxes that spoil the vine (see Song of Sol. 2:15). Once you make the first compromise, it's easy to make the second, then the third, then the next, and the next.

When do we outgrow temptation? I asked Dr. Paul Rees, one of my heroes, "Paul, you're a veteran of the cross, and a noble gentleman with an impeccable reputation. Are you ever tempted?"

He replied, "I'm constantly tempted. At my age, I'm continually tempted."

True honesty stems from an accurate realization of what we are and what we need to become.

That encouraged me to realize a man of his stature— then 87 years old—was willing to admit the longevity of temptation. Misery loves company and so does temptation. Honesty is a willingness to admit the problem and seek the Lord's help in overcoming it.

Fortunately, that help is always available. I remember the example of my good friend, Bob Pierce. I was with him in a hotel room one night in Tokyo. It was late and he was already in bed, but I heard him praying. Though sound asleep, he was praying out loud for the people in Japan to which he was ministering. In my estimation, it takes an honest man to pour out his spirit to God for the welfare of others while sleeping. That goal could wake anyone from a spiritual slumber.

Obviously I would never claim to be perfect. There are not a few dogs nipping at the heels of my conscience. Confessing them with you, right here in these pages, might be the prod I need to provoke myself unto love and good works, as we're admonished in Hebrews 10:24.

Too often it seems I pour out so much energy preaching a strong message I seemingly don't have strength left to put it into practice. I'm always talking to people about the importance of studying the Word and find myself neglecting it far too often. And I have a good message about:

God's four answers to prayer:

1. No, not yet

2. No, I love you too much

3. Yes, I'm glad you asked.

4. Yes, and there's more to come.

I preach this with effectiveness, but I don't always practice the message. I hope my willingness to admit these problems is a large part of their solution.

MORAL COMPASS

Keeping our bearings in the moral wilderness requires a good compass. For several years now I've given lectures on four points for helping individuals develop and use their leadership skills. Let me review these here in the form of a moral compass.

Christian Survival Compass

North—Keep your eyes fixed on Christ—the only true point of reference.

East—Pray. Let each sunrise in the east remind you to start the day in contact with the Creator.

South—Tackle your problems. You can't run, you've got to face them sometime. South of Israel is the great Negev desert—the vast wasteland in which the Israelites wandered for 40 years because they refused to face their problems.

West—Control your passions for money, sex and pride. Just as the sun sets in the west, so will our potential for the future if we don't rule the flesh. Paul says, "Let not the sun go down upon your wrath" (Eph. 4:26, *KJV*). To which I add, Let it not go down on pride, lust or greed. Put them out quickly.

THE SOURCE OF HONESTY

True honesty stems from an accurate realization of what we are and what we need to become.

King Solomon acknowledged, "I *am* a little child; I do not know *how* to go out or come in" (1 Kings 3:7). Jeremiah admitted, "*It is* not in man who walks to direct his own steps" (Jer. 10:23) and "The heart *is* deceitful above all *things*, and desperately wicked" (Jer. 17:9). Christ Himself recognized, "I can of Myself do nothing" (John 5:30). Paul taught "All have sinned" (Rom. 3:23) and "In me . . . dwelleth no good thing" (Rom. 7:18, *KJV*). These are not the admissions of a godless heathen, they're the words of a king, prophet, apostle and Savior.

But fortunately we're not condemned to live with this state of character dishonesty forever. Look at the transformation that's available. "I can do all things through Christ" (Phil. 4:13). "With God all things are possible" (Matt. 19:26). "He who believes in Me, the works that I do he will do also; and greater *works* than these he will do" (John 14:12).

In my estimation, this conversion from beast to believer lies at the heart of what makes a person honest. But all it takes is a divine miracle. No wonder the world of business has so much trouble with this issue.

PROFESSIONAL HONESTY

I appreciate the insight of my friend, Frank Goble, author of *Excellence In Leadership*. He recounts a number of important principles and examples from the world of business:

"Joe Batten, advocate of tough-minded management, believes that we must 'blast the fallacy that you must compromise integrity to run a truly profitable business or home—this is an absolute lie and an inexcusable fallacy.' I made a similar remark to a professor of management at one of the nation's leading graduate schools of business. His retort was, 'I doubt if many of our graduate students will buy that.' The prevalent concept for many Americans, including many executives who should know better, is: Be successful or be honest.

"No one can deny that there are many successful people, at least financially, who are not very honest. And yet, the study of excellent leadership reveals that integrity is an essential quality. It is exceedingly difficult to achieve success in handling people, over the long span, without it. Arthur Gordon, writing for *Reader's Digest*, says, 'Year after year businessmen study college records, screen applicants, and offer special inducement to proven people. What are they after, really? Brains? Energy? Know how? These things are desirable, sure. But they will carry a man so far. If he is to move to the top and be entrusted with command decisions, there must be a plus factor, something that takes mere ability and doubles or trebles its effectiveness. To describe this magic characteristic there is only one word: integrity.'

"In 1930, J. Taylor was vice president of Jewel Tea Co., in line for the presidency and receiving the then princely salary of $33,000 a year. A group of bankers asked Jewel Tea to lend Taylor to them for a few months to see if he could save Club Aluminum Products from bankruptcy. It was the bottom of the Great Depression. Millions were out of work, and many companies and banks were failing. Taylor found Club Aluminum $400,000 in debt and losing more each month. Any three creditors were in a position to throw the company into bankruptcy.

"Taylor made a daring decision to leave his secure, well-paying job with Jewel Tea, borrow $6,100 and take over the presidency of Club Aluminum. His starting salary was $6,000 a year. One of his first moves was to devise some guiding principles for the company. He called them 'The Four-Way Test' and years later assigned the copyright to Rotary International. Here are the four principles:

1. Is it the truth?
2. Is it fair to all concerned?
3. Will it build goodwill and better friendships?
4. Will it be beneficial to all concerned?

"Taylor's associates agreed to abide by the test, and everyone in the company was told about it and encouraged to use it in all their dealings.

"The advertising department had been billing Club Aluminum ware as 'the greatest cookware in the world.' Under the new policy these superlatives were eliminated, and advertising sought to tell only the facts about the product. The company's sales strategy had been to try to load dealers with as large an inventory as possible on the theory that this would force them to push the product harder. Now salesmen were taught to consider the best interests of the dealers. On one occasion the company turned down a desperately needed order for 50,000 aluminum utensils because the buyer wanted to sell them at a cut price which would not be fair to other dealers. The result was that Club Aluminum won the confidence and respect of all its dealers, and this feeling was passed on to customers. Sales climbed steadily. At a time when many other companies were failing, Club Aluminum was able to pay back its $400,000 debt in 5 years, with interest, and during the next 15 years went on to distribute over one million dollars in stock dividends.

"Norman Jaspan, head of a firm specializing in detection and prevention of white-collar crime, says, 'Dishonesty starts from the top and works downward. Show me a half-dozen honest key supervisors who know their business, and I'll show you a thousand honest employees. Show me a couple of executives who are dishonest, disinterested, and disloyal, and I will show you a thousand dishonest employees.'"[1]

SUPER BOWL OF SCANDAL

In the fall of 1986, Ivan Boesky rocked Wall Street and the

world with his own private interpretation of corporate honesty. *Newsweek* termed it "The Super Bowl of Scandal."[2] Mr. Boesky thought he could rewrite 50 years of ethics about trading on the stock market. He wound up receiving the largest fine ever imposed by the Securities and Exchange Commission.

Only a year previous he was cancelling at least two commandments in one speech at the University of California's school of business administration. "Greed is all right, by the way. I want you to know that. I think greed is healthy. You can be greedy and still feel good about yourself," he told the students in a commencement address.[3]

There were those who adamantly disagreed with Ivan Boesky. To use privileged information about a corporation's takeover intentions in order to extort tens of millions of dollars from the stockholders simply wasn't honest. And the penalty caught up with Mr. Boesky. Federal investigators charged him with one felony count plus $100 million in fines and restitution payments. Honesty still has its merits.

I'm reminded of the Aesop fable about the ass and the lion's skin. "An ass found a Lion's skin, dressed himself up in it, and went among the flocks and herds frightening the animals out of their wits. At last he met his master, and tried to frighten him, but the man, seeing the long ears sticking out, knew him at once and, taking a stick, beat him until he realized that although he was dressed in a Lion's skin, he was really only an ass. The moral is obvious: Don't pretend to be what you are not."

How many of us pretend to be more powerful, more wealthy, more attractive, more famous than we actually are? If some "master" doesn't beat us in private, without a doubt, we can count on finding ourselves eventually getting beaten in public.

DISHONEST FAT

I don't recommend we tackle the problem of honesty with the same spirit that beleaguers plastic surgeons. These professionals have a lot to offer people with deformities and severe injuries. But recently I read about new procedures that seem to attract a great deal of interest from people whose honesty I question. For a long time we've known about implants that allow the creation of a more shapely figure. But now there are two more methods for making us appear to be what we are not. Suction-assisted lipectomy (SAL) allows the surgeon to vacuum fat out of the body. Then autologous fat grafting is the removal of fat from one area for the padding of another.

Is this the honest answer to weight problems and beauty care? It seems 477,700 patients thought so in 1984 when they turned to the plastic surgeon for "strictly aesthetic reasons." The article I saw cautioned: "Surgery should be considered a last resort. Complications—including massive infection and even death have been associated with these surgeries."[4] But how many people want to correct the effects without making an honest attempt to solve the problems in health care and other areas of their lives?

AN HONEST LOOK AT OUR CHALLENGES

In chapter 2 we saw the scope of work that needs to be done in the Two-Thirds World. But how prepared are we to serve?

In the days ahead our leaders will increasingly become world citizens. And there will be global demands as never before in fulfilling the Great Commission.

Let's take a look at our need for cultural understanding

in other parts of the world. What seems "honest" to us in America may be viewed as upside down to someone on the other side of the world.

Cultural integrity is a must. For example, in our Western society it is unthinkable for a man to walk into a church with his hat on and his shoes off. In the Near East it is equally unthinkable for a man to enter a mosque with his shoes on and his hat off.

Even the most unscientific prejudices must be respected. A missionary who does not agree with the teaching of Islam but is working among Muslims must not stop a farmer along the road and ask him about the expected yield of his field. To do so would not be a sign of friendliness as it would be in Iowa. Rather, it would be an insult, the equal of calling the man a blasphemer, for "only Allah knows the future" our Muslim friend would say.

Not everyone shares our same set of values.

For example, the Muslim view of winning others through the sword is seen quite clearly at the inception of Islam. Mohammed met resistance from the people of Mecca and was forced to flee to Medina. He gathered fighting men around him, and there was war between the people of Mecca and Medina. Mohammed finally entered Mecca peacefully, but then he began to gather more troops to wage further war. When Muslim men began to falter in their commitment to that kind of war, revelations came from God, according to Mohammed, to the effect that they should not hesitate to take up the sword and to fight in the name of God. To die in battle is to go to paradise. To convert pagans by the force of the sword is a virtue, Mohammed maintained.

It is of interest to note that in Islamic teaching (not in the Koran but in its traditions) it is held that Jesus Christ is going to return; that He will come as a Muslim; that He will be used of God to convert the whole world to Islam and that He is going to marry, have children and work for 40 years. When He dies, he is going to be buried in the tomb already prepared for Him beside the tomb of the prophet Mohammed in Medina.

Mohammed also believed that there was a verse in the Scriptures that prophesied his own coming. This grew out of a corrupted Arabic text in which the word *paraclete* from the Greek was misspelled and came out looking like

---

We need God's help to be completely honest in every relationship so that we are better capable of transcending the differences that exist among Homo sapiens.

Mohammed's name in Arabic. When he sought to investigate this with Christian scholars, they pointed out that it really was not his name but another word brought over from the Greek into Arabic. It was at this point that he accused the Christians of changing the Scriptures. So, there is a tremendous battlegound in the whole area of revelation.

The Muslims believe there are four inspired books: the Torah of Moses, the Zabur of David, the Injil of Jesus and the Quran (Koran) given to Mohammed. But they do not admit that any valid copy or translation of the previous three exist as they were originally given.

This makes it extremely difficult to deal with a thoroughly indoctrinated Muslim on the basis of the Old and New Testaments because his mind is closed. He avoids the issue by saying, "Well, you can't trust those scriptures because . . . "

The because is that they aren't "honest" in the eyes of another culture. So what can we do to increase the level of understanding between peoples of highly divergent value systems?

We who identify with the WASP (White Anglo-Saxon Protestant) community are often unwilling to face the fact, for example, that the white race is not supreme. We have difficulty in accepting the truth that all humankind stand equal—as sinners and as servants—before a just and righteous God.

We need to confess our sin in this regard. Facing the fact is the important start. Asking God's forgiveness should follow. We need God's help to be completely honest in every relationship so that we are better capable of transcending the differences that exist among Homo sapiens. Only thus will hosts of people for whom Christ died be reached for Him in this generation.

So the church of the West, especially the United States, has lost much of its credibility because much of the Third World considers missionary endeavor from this area as part of an oppressive structure. Those in the Third World became suspicious because they perceived the U.S. church as being accommodated to Western cultural values and to Western power structures.

Missionaries were not completely innocent either. They often seemed to go out as if "marching off to war" with a "we-know-everything, we-can-do-nothing-wrong" attitude. Their hymns were often military in character, their evangelism was aggressive and their money was irresistible.

It may be that today we are still perpetuating the same Western theological parochialism with our economic power, although gratefully it is lessening. Because of the might and superiority of the West, those in the Third World often have difficulty in identifying with Western missions.

Rather than perpetuating such attitudes, we need a more relevant theological perspective. This is desperately needed to enable the church in the Third World to attain its selfhood and to realistically relate to the social issues that are tearing many of these societies apart.

What is there about America—and Americans—that makes us feel superior to our brothers in Asia or Africa or Latin America? I know this is a generalization, but it is too often true to be ignored. This superiority attitude creeps out in so many ways that seem innocuous to the offender but are deeply hurtful to the offended. For example, we are apt to call our friends in the national church in Tanzania or Korea or Bolivia the "natives" or "native Christians." Immediately this calls to mind half-naked "savages," head-hunters or illiterate peasants. These are *people*. They would much prefer to be called "nationals" or "national Christians"—or Tanzanians or Koreans or Bolivians. Even when they do not comment on this problem, they cringe inwardly under our patronizing attitude.

Again, this attitude is often reflected in our exported Western-styled literature for Christians, with little appreciation or understanding of the culture, ethnic background and history of the people we seek to reach. It is increasingly important that literature be written and produced by people who have this background.

These people in other cultures are our Christian brothers and friends. Although they may carefully note and keenly resent our insensitivities, most of them would never be so ungracious as to bring them to our attention!

No American traveler abroad would likely admit to

being a part of the infamous "ugly American" image. And perhaps most are not guilty of the gross blunders charged in that term. Yet we are closely observed by Christians in the younger churches abroad—in what we so casually call the "mission field"—that is *home* to them, and an attitude of condescension too often shows through.

There is no question that the stigma far too often attached to Western missions is a realistic problem that must be faced. Horace Fenton points out this condition: "I believe that the Latin American Mission cannot be really effective in its evangelistic objective until fully rooted in Latin America . . . . There are only a limited number of Latins who will continue to honor us with their membership in our mission unless there are basic and deep changes in our whole structure."[5]

These realities demand a sense of cultural honesty about ourselves and our place in the world community. But this larger view of honesty has to stem from a smaller seed. How can we be honest about our race and our culture if we are not first honest about ourselves and our own personal values?

SUMMING UP

1. Watch how you handle the money of others. God expects His leaders—young and old—to understand the importance of financial accountability.

2. Remember that our lives are transparent before the eyes of others. People notice the drinks we order, the movies we watch, the books we read, even when we think no one is watching.

3. Chart your course with the Christian Survival Compass.

4. Remember Herbert Taylor's Four Way Test.

5. Be honest in your concern for the needs of our brothers in other lands.

We've reviewed the subject from fact, fable, foible, fallacy and farce. I can only hope at this point that your conclusions are fair and honest. The remainder of this century and the decades beyond have an honest chance if you who receive the torch of leadership are willing to give it one. For then and only then can we experience the inner confidence to display the next great quality of leadership explained in chapter 6.

Chapter Six

COURAGE
Swimming Against the Current

What enables you as a
Christian leader to
make this upstream
struggle for Jesus Christ
is God's ability to part the
waters and reverse the
currents. Christ promised a
true believer, "out of his
belly shall flow rivers of living
water."

*"Tell a man he is brave
and you help him become so."*
Thomas Carlyle[1]

As challenges of honesty, enthusiasm, motivation, goal setting and commitment cascade down on the heads of a new generation of leaders, the natural instinct may be to turn away from the onrush and float downstream with the other drifters. But like the great salmon of the Pacific Northwest, the urge to serve the greater needs of posterity drives exceptional individuals upstream against all threats to personal comfort and safety. So it is with a leader. Surmounting obstacles demands yet another quality of character—*courage.*

Our past Christian leaders were distinguished by the courage of their convictions, courage in their public witnessing, courage to proclaim the truth no matter what the cost may have been, courage in their travels. They were intrepid.

There was Willis Shenk who lost his life flying to Alaska to evangelize for Youth for Christ. He challenged the largest state in the union with a small aircraft and lost—physically. But I have to believe the impression made by his sincerity on those who expected to hear from him that evening will live forever.

I think of Billy Graham at Forest Home Christian Conference grounds in 1949. He was questioning whether or not he could preach the Bible completely. This question drew him into a long night of prayer and wrestling with the Lord. Should he preach what people wanted to hear and expected to hear? Or should he step out in faith and preach what he knew he must?

Many congregations want personal comfort and instant satisfaction. It takes courage to preach service toward the needs of others, coupled with patience and longsuffering.

Finally after long hours of walking and meditating, he said in essence to God, "From this point on I will take your Word at face value exactly the way you've given it to me, and I'll never question it again." And he never has. That's why he could say all through his preaching ministry, "the Bible says, the Bible says." This phrase has marked his ministry. It was a courageous step on his part. No matter what the critics would say, he would stick with the Word of God as the authoritative, inerrant, will of God.

OUR LOCAL CHALLENGE

If you are a pastor, your challenge is much the same today. People want to hear something that will silence the guilt they feel about neglecting the Word of God. But it takes courage to preach what they need to hear about repentance and righteousness. More and more Christians are interested in new age "spiritual technology" and "soul physics"—messages that do not require allegiance to the church or loss of personal power. But it takes courage to teach Christ crucified, Master of our destiny. Many congregations want personal comfort and instant satisfaction. It takes courage to preach service toward the needs of others, coupled with patience and longsuffering.

One way to gain the skills needed today in the home congregation is to look at the skills exemplified in the past from Christian missionaries overseas. Though the places may have been strange and far away, the lessons are near and familiar to the challenge of today's pluralistic society.

OF COBBLERS AND MARTYRS

The period of the modern missionary movement goes back to William Carey, who had the courage to leave his cobbler's bench in Britain late in the eighteenth century and travel to India. His exemplary life and zealous ministry in India seemed to spark the concerned Christian world to new effort in missions. Mission societies began to spring up with the exclusive purpose of getting people to the field and raising the funds to keep them there.

Carey had an unparalleled influence in India. There he founded the Baptist Church movement, translated the Scriptures into four major Indian languages, began what is now the largest college and seminary in that nation and was editor of what has since become the largest newspaper in India.

Missionaries such as David Livingstone, Adoniram Judson, Mary Slessor, Hudson Taylor, and others went where no other white person had ever gone before. They were, in the fullest sense of the word, pioneers.

Many of them were martyrs. They died early deaths as they cut a swath through the wilds and jungles, and went to places where the gospel had never been preached.

TO LOVE A MURDERER

Surely one of the most courageous men of this century is Ugandan Anglican Bishop Festo Kivengere, resident of a country that took the unbridled anger and fury of the half-crazed, self-appointed president-for-life, Idi Amin.

For eight long years, 1971-'79, blood flowed from the innocent bodies of men, women and children. Amin was no respecter of persons. A classic example of a paranoiac, he saw the enemy behind every tree, and each threat to him, imagined or real, was disposed of in the most horrible fashion imaginable.

Amin's infamous State Research Bureau kept tabs on these "enemies," and through its sophisticated underground network it was able to kill, maim and destroy large numbers of Uganda's best and brightest. He used every means possible to perpetuate his power and his crimes.

During Uganda's darkest hours, our World Vision teams interviewed grieving families. We would hear stories of how five to six family members had been picked up in the dead of night, thrown into the trunks of cars, and taken out and shot. After we had heard literally hundreds of these stories, it was difficult to separate truth from what might have been fiction, because there came a point where they were one and the same.

During this Ugandan holocaust if any one man had cause for anger and retribution, it was Bishop Kivengere. His archbishop was ambushed and killed by Amin's troops.

Festo's flock of faithful, Spirit-filled men, women and children were gunned down, knived, butchered or raped. Yet, by the mercy of God, Festo was ultimately able to say, "I love Idi Amin." He soon wrote a book by that same title.[2]

MIRACLE AT THE MOSQUE

Because of his courage, Festo is in great demand everywhere as a conference and missions speaker. For several years a refugee from troubled Uganda, he tells the following story:

Shortly before the murder of Anglican Archbishop Luwum in 1977, Festo and a colleague of his were holding meetings in one of the universities in Uganda. Some of the students thought it would be marvelous if these men could share their Christian testimony in a Muslim mosque. The students courageously made the request to the proper authorities and amazingly their request was granted and arrangements were finalized.

The leaders of the mosque invited the two men to speak there on their holy day, a Friday. Six hundred of them, upon entering the mosque, took off their shoes and listened for a solid hour to the message concerning Jesus Christ from the two evangelists.

During the service the evangelists detected some shuffling of the curtains alongside the mosque and subsequently learned that about 200 women were eavesdropping to hear the message of Jesus Christ. Some of these women asked permission of the leaders to see if they might enter the mosque to hear these men, something unheard-of in that part of the world. Permission granted, they entered, fully veiled, and for another hour, they, along with the men, listened to the gospel preached by two African Christians.

FIRST CHRISTIAN CHURCH IN AFGHANISTAN

Another courageous illustration is from my own experience. Back in 1972 I had the privilege of visiting with my dear friend, Dr. J. Christy Wilson, in Kabul, Afghanistan. He went there many years earlier to teach English to government leaders in this closed Muslim nation, considered quite likely the most hard-core Muslim nation in the world.

As a result of his leadership, a community of believers resident in the capital city from many Western nations was formed. Ambassadors, government officials from the various embassies in the capital, teachers and others formed the core of this small Christian group. Dr. Wilson served as pastor.

Obviously no Afghan could be a member of this group, for if an Afghan becomes a Christian, the believer will either be put to death or at the very least expelled from the country. Yet, as a result of the witness of Christians from other parts of the world, several score of Afghans have committed themselves to Christ and have become secret believers. They are known to each other, but would not dare publicly identify themselves, upon threat of death.

On that visit I preached the dedication sermon at the first Christian church ever constructed in Afghanistan. Though it was built for the European Christian community, it was a great testimony for Christ there in the midst of this Islamic stronghold.

Some two years after the church's dedication, it was destroyed by government decree for fear of its pervasive influence. But as an outgrowth and extension of its work, there is an increasing ministry underground in that closed country. Many Afghan believers bravely share their faith in secret with family and friends week after week.

A ROPE OF HOPE

A veteran Korean Christian told me an inspiring story not long ago about how the gospel first came to his country. Back in the early 1880s, there were, among others, three Korean workmen laboring in northern China. The gospel had recently come to that part of China and many Chinese had come to a knowledge of Christ through the efforts of missionaries. Some of these Chinese Christians, in turn, shared their gospel witness with these three Koreans, who eventually acknowledged Christ as Savior and Lord.

These Koreans were eager to bring the gospel back into their own land of Korea, where there had been no Christians nor Christian witness. At the time it was against the law to bring other religions into Korea. These three men obtained copies of the Chinese Bible, which uses the same characters as the Korean language. They decided they would try to smuggle a copy of the Bible into their country. They drew straws to see who would have the privilege of being the first to bring a copy of the Bible to their people.

The first man sought to bury a copy of the Scriptures in his belongings. It took him many days' journey by foot to the border where he was apprehended by the guards. They searched his luggage and found the Bible, and as a result he was killed. After many days word came back to the two remaining men that their friend had lost his life.

The second man, who had drawn the second longest straw, tore pages from his Bible and sought to have those separate pages buried in his knapsack among his belongings. He in turn took the long journey to the border, was searched, and again the Scriptures were found. He was beheaded.

Word filtered back to the third man. He was more determined than ever to bring the gospel into his own land. So, ingeniously, he tore his Bible apart page by page and wrapped each page separately to form a rope. Then he wrapped all his belongings with this homemade rope. When he came to the border, the guards asked him to unwrap his belongings. Unsuspected, he was admitted into his country, and later, very meticulously, he untied the rope, ironed out each page and reassembled the Scriptures. Then he began to preach Christ wherever he went.

THIRST FOR RIGHTEOUSNESS

Probably of all the churches in the Third World, none is more exciting, faster growing or more effective than the church in Korea. There were no church buildings left standing in Seoul, when the capital city was leveled during the Korean conflict in the early 1950s. Many of the Christians struggled down from North Korea as refugees and suffered severe persecution. Today in the city of Seoul there are over 6,000 separate evangelical Protestant churches! In most of them it is standing room only.

On a visit to Korea some time ago, my wife, Dorothy, and I wanted to visit a church I had heard so much about, located in a great plaza often used for various national events. On this plaza is an amazing church, pastored by Pastor Paul Yongi Cho.

Twenty years ago, Pastor Cho's mother-in-law urged him to begin a gospel ministry. He did so in a tent in the city of Seoul. The ministry grew by leaps and bounds and now the new church building seats over 20,000 people!

Every Sunday morning there are four worship

services—each one filled to capacity with worshippers. The Sunday afternoon service is a celebration service of witness, testimony and song. And there would be another capacity crowd for the two evening evangelistic services! Think of it, all services, every Sunday, filled, making an aggregate total of tens of thousands of people in those Sunday services! And this is only one church!

One of the most spectacular things happening in Korea in recent years is the revival going on among the Republic of Korea (ROK) military personnel. This movement has not received much attention in the world press, but the Spirit of God has been working dramatically, according to one of my young friends from the World Vision Childcare Programs. It is estimated that between 30 and 40 percent of the ROK troops have accepted Christ and are involved in the process of Christian growth.

In addition, Korea is one of the few nations in Asia with a network of Christian radio stations, which beam throughout South Korea and into communist North Korea. The stations are sponsored by evangelical churches and missions.

Now, how many such groups and churches in Korea would be "tied together" in the Lord were it not for the courage of that third Bible messenger and his "rope of hope"?

LAND OF PERSECUTION

Such exploits are not confined to Korea. For many years Colombia was known as the land of persecution. The struggling Protestant church was under severe persecution.

A number of years ago I was sharing in a missionary conference at the Maranatha Bible Conference in western

Michigan. One day I was having lunch with David Howard, who was then a missionary to Colombia. Dave has since served as director for three great Urbana Student Conferences of the Inter-Varsity Christian Fellowship and is Director of the World Evangelism Fellowship.

Over lunch Dave sadly related to me the martyrdom of two of his dear young pastor friends who were killed in Colombia, merely because they were leaders in their respective evangelical churches. He knew them intimately and was deeply moved by the fact that they gave their lives willingly as martyrs.

But look what their courage helped secure. Today gospel films are being shown in Colombian theaters, gospel radio broadcasts are being held weekly on the national radio networks, churches are wide open and filled, and it is possible without harassment in most places to freely pass out gospel literature and tracts in the parks of the cities.

SHIRTSLEEVE SAINTS

It would be easy to dismiss such courageous exploits as the untouchable conquests of a few rare superstars. But that would be a mistake. Today's leaders are made of the same leadership cloth. I simply urge you to seize the torch!

Consider my friend Pete Johnson. Pete is a fellow member at my home church. He is a handyman, plumber, carpenter and builder. On several different occasions he has gone to Irian Jaya in Indonesia to help the missionary community there with various building programs. By so doing he has unleashed the missionaries so they can carry on their evangelism and training ministries. Pete has courageously given himself for work they ordinarily would have to do. While in no way theologically trained, Pete is using his special skills and gifts in an important and glorious ministry.

Then I think of Denny and Jeanne Grindall from Seattle, Washington. Denny and Jeanne wrestled for some time with the issue of what the Lord wanted them to do in their retirement years. They are warm, committed Christians, and the love of Christ shines through their entire beings, but they both admit, "We are just ordinary people . . . very ordinary."

The Grindalls decided to take a journey, a simple tourist trip, for several months, leaving their successful florist business in Seattle. While they were in Kenya, East Afica, they were taken by missionary friends to the nomadic Masai people. They found these people were living a primitive life; the death rate was extremely high and life expectancy was low. The Grindalls found chickens, pigs and other animals living with humans in the little mud huts. Together Denny and Jeanne determined they would go back to live among these fascinating people and work together with them in programs of community development.

The Grindalls decided to assist the Masai in learning how to obtain vitally necessary water, building pigpens, and developing sanitation facilities. They wanted to share their knowledge in horticulture and give guidance out of their experience. Today, six months out of every year this post middle-aged couple lives among the Masai and are beautifully accepted by these formerly nomadic people.

The once unsanitary huts have been cleaned out, the quality of health has improved greatly and people are living longer. Children are no longer suffering from malnutrition, and the lives of whole communities have been tremendously improved through the loving care and concern of these warm Christians from the Pacific Northwest. With all of this Denny and Jeanne have borne a tremendous Christian witness, and scores of Masais have come to Christ.

The Grindalls' example illustrates what any congregation can contribute to the needs of the world or the needs of their community through *courage*.

COURAGEOUS ROLES AND RULES FOR WOMEN

We touched on the impact of the women's movement in chapter 3 while exploring The End of Female Passivity. This subject becomes a double-edged razor. It can cut through the restrictive cords holding women back from meaningful advancement in society and in the Church. But these new roles for women can also sever the delicate stitches that protect society from family decay and sexual abuse. Handling such a sharp issue demands courage of conviction and courage of action. Every new leader, man or woman, will face them.

Few concerns have greater impact on the roles of leader, follower, missionary and peoples. Misunderstanding about whether men and women are created beings with clearly defined roles or evolutionary creatures with shifting responsibilities will color every facet of the coming century. One false social move and an emerging leader may alienate half of his or her followers. One false doctrinal move and a new leader alienates church establishment. The need for courage is obvious.

According to Eleanor Smeal, president of the National Organization of Women (NOW)—whose politics I disagree with, but whose statistics I'm prepared to accept—women in 1966 made up 3 percent of law schools, 8 percent of medical schools, 1 percent of engineering schools and virtually 0 percent of divinity schools. After 20 years of feminist activity, women represent about 40 percent of law students, 30 percent of medical students, 25 percent of engineering students and about 60 percent of seminary students in the Protestant denominations. "It's a revolution. We're still working on the Catholic priesthood. That will fall," added Smeal.[3]

Since women's perceptions about themselves as created beings have changed, so have their perceptions about that which they create. In-laws, husbands, sons and daughters, become unwitting victims of unfulfilled people.

According to figures released in 1986 by the Census Bureau, nearly one-fourth of children under age 18 live with only one parent. The 23 percent of children in such families is up from only 9 percent in 1960. Over 2.2 million couples now live together as unmarried partners. That represents 4.1 percent of all couples in the nation. *Glamour* magazine polled 800 readers and discovered that 76 percent of them do not think marriage is a prerequisite for having children.[4]

Close to 20 million Americans have been executed by abortionists since radical feminists convinced the Supreme Court in 1973 to permit abortion on demand. That figure represents 10 times the total number of Americans lost in all of our nation's wars. Every day 4,300 new unborns fall victim.[5]

But despite drawbacks, the groundswell of concern for women's rights and responsibilities has its positive implications for the Church in the decades ahead.

THE NEW CHURCH WOMAN

For most of the twentieth century, the majority of evangelicals assumed women should not be ordained for ministry or become church leaders. We all labored under some rather narrow interpretations of selected passages of Scripture. A wider vision is much more prevalent today.

Our next generation of church leaders will be training female recruits and answering to female superiors in ever increasing numbers. Symbolic of this was the 1986 election of a woman as the commanding general of the Salvation Army. This growing trend calls for its own brand of courage. Courage on the part of men to face change and relinquish responsibility. Courage on the part of women to blaze new trails and prove themselves in new positions.

In a survey conducted in 1984, *Christianity Today* reported that the percentage of women enrolled in seminaries had increased twice as fast as that of the total student population. Their census of 34 responding schools was one-fifth female, up from less than one tenth in 1965. [6]

The chairperson of our World Vision International Board, Reverend Doctor Roberta Hestenes, is herself a graduate of Fuller Theological Seminary, an ordained Presbyterian minister and now president of Eastern College. "I travel the world, and I have been amazed and pleased that Christian men, when they are exposed to Christian women as partners in ministry, are much more accepting than the stereotypes would suggest," she recently observed in *Christianity Today*. [7]

The history behind this change in the role of women in church goes back to the Radical Reformation, the Quakers, and in the first feminist movement, which arose out of the movement to abolish slavery in the early and mid nineteenth century. Many mainline, holiness and Pentecostal churches had been ordaining women as elders and ministers for decades before the contemporary feminist movement began in the 1960s and '70s. The Presbyterian church, for example, started the movement to ordain women as early as the 1930s and 1950s.

These organizations had the courage to reexamine old assumptions about the Bible in the light of new understanding. The dividing line between those who believe that women were created to serve the ministers and those who believe women were created to serve as ministers takes the following path. When familiar texts like 1 Corinthians 14:34, and 1 Timothy 2:8-15, women's silence, are placed alongside less familiar texts like 2 Kings 22:13-20, Huldah speaking the word of the Lord, and Acts 2:17,18, 21:9, women's ministry of prophecy, a reappraisal often begins to occur.

Culturally, there has been a temptation to take a particular form of the nuclear family as it emerged in America after World War II and make it the biblical norm for all Christian families. The image of the ideal suburban family, with the woman as full-time homemaker, is a model of short duration throughout Church history. Scripture gets used, in this case, to support a view of the family shaped by culture. For instance, black women have always worked, and the church has never really debated whether the poor black woman must work. Ruth worked. Priscilla made tents alongside Aquila. The biblical patterns are much more varied.

I'm grateful to Dr. Hestenes for the preceeding assessment from history, the Bible and culture. Her keen observations are set forth in a book entitled *The Next Step: Women in a Divided Church.*[8] I endorse its courageous contents.

A REVIEW IN COURAGE

1. Look to the courage of our fellow servants far away to learn more about conquering the problems at home.

2. Love the murderer, hate the murders. Bishop Festo Kivengere of Uganda demonstrates the courage it takes to love God in a climate of hate.

3. Hold on to the rope of hope. Do we braid the Word of God into a form that no one else can take away?

4. Remember the "shirtsleeve saints". Here are everyday Christians doing once-in-a-life-time actions day in and day out.

5. Respect the new roles for women. Be ready to take advantage of the new leadership opportunities now available to you within the fellowship of *all* believers.

We opened this chapter with a reference to the Pacific salmon and their valiant struggle upstream each year. If they didn't make the effort, the species would perish. We've explored many parallels from Uganda, Korea and other Christian spawning grounds.

What enables you as a Christian leader to make this upstream struggle for Jesus Christ is God's ability to part the waters and reverse the currents. Christ promised a true believer, "out of his heart will flow rivers of living water" (John 7:38). As long as you and I maintain the flow of these spiritual currents, we can move against the mightiest of floods. All it takes is courage and the ability to act on that courage—as we will discover in chapter 7.

Chapter Seven

DECISION MAKING
Ready, Aim
Now What?

All of us are conscious
of the desire to put off
deciding. But few of us
are fully aware of the
degree to which habitual
inability to make decisions
interferes with the
realization of our full
potential and the attainment
of our goals in life.

*"Between the great things we cannot do
and the small things we will not do
the danger is that we shall do nothing."*
Adolphe Monod[1]

Trained, equipped and authorized to use deadly force—
what are some of the decision-making guidelines a
police officer must master before pulling the trigger on
another human being? This question intrigued me. So I
gathered some information from a lieutenant involved in
training recruits at a large metropolitan police academy.
The split second frenzy of an incident doesn't leave time to
think about *how* to make a decision. There is only time to
decide. This life- and death-training is extremely revealing.
But before we examine it, let's take a look at some early
decisions I was involved in that might have benefited from
a steadier hand on the trigger.

One poor decision I made back in the days of my service with Youth for Christ was when we used something
we called the Talking Christian Horse. We asked how
many apostles there were, and he would paw the ground
12 times. We asked him how many close disciples Jesus
had, and he would whinny three times. It sure got people's

attention, until he had an accident on the floor of the platform in a rally at Muskegon, Michigan. That incident broke up the meeting and ended our horse testimonials.

I remember my friend Roy McKeown and his interview with the writer of "The Old Rugged Cross," George Bernard, at a convention at Winona Lake. In the interview Mr. Bernard was talking about his first wife when he said, "Yes, she passed away about four years ago." Roy, not thinking what was said, replied, "Isn't that wonderful!"

In those days you went out onto the platform wearing a lighted bow tie. There'd be a battery in your pocket, and when you walked out with a great big grin on your face you'd flicker the lights. That would certainly be a mistake today, and I'm not so sure it wasn't one back then.

TWO WORDS OF ADVICE

There once was a young man who was given the nod to become president of a small town bank, a big responsibility in any community. He had risen through the ranks of clerk, cashier and vice president. One day he approached the feisty old president of the bank who had been there for a generation. The young man said, "Sir, as you know, I have been named your successor as president of the bank, and I'd be grateful for any counsel you can give to me."

The old man said, "Son, sit down. I've got two words for you, only two words."

"What are they, sir?"

"Right decisions," said the veteran.

The young man thought a moment and said, "That's very helpful, sir, but how does one go about making right decisions?"

The outgoing president replied, "One word— experience."

Upon further reflection, the young man said, "Well, that too is helpful, but how does one go about gaining experience?"

The old man smiled and added, "Two words, son, two words—wrong decisions."

DECISION MENTORS

I received a great deal of help in learning to avoid making wrong decisions. Three people come to mind immediately. First there was a pair of brothers I worked for, Pat and Bernie Zondervan. Extremely successful businessmen, a bit older than me, I joined them in the early days of their publishing careers. The Zondervans taught me to make pass-or-fail decisions on scores of manuscripts. Each decision affected the economic well-being of the company and often, the entire career of an author. We all learned to ponder quickly.

My other mentor was Bob Cook, past president of Youth for Christ and King's College in New York. He probably taught me more about decision making than any other person. I'm in constant correspondence with him even now.

Bob Cook emphasized two important principles. Rule number 1—make the decision. Then don't look back after you've made it. Move ahead. And rule 2 says, If you're in doubt, wait. But once you've determined the way to go, move forward with speed.

TO SHOOT OR NOT TO SHOOT

Regarding the police training I mentioned earlier, there's a great deal to consider in a short time when making a life-

and-death decision with the trigger. Deadly force shooting policy recognizes two main categories: self-defense and fleeing felons. There are few restrictions on an officer when it comes to self-defense or the lives of those in the immediate area. Where stray bullets or missed shots may fall is about all they have to decide. When pursuing a felon, decisiveness becomes even more essential. Is the target, *in fact,* a felon? Will that person's escape, *in fact,* impose a threat to the community? What is the background beyond the target where bullets may strike? And how old is the felon?

That last question struck me as a bit academic and out of place. But I soon learned its importance. After using deadly force, an officer must stand before a Use of Force Board and answer these same questions. Requiring an officer to collect and store cold facts before making a hot decision, helps protect against irrational behavior. But it's a practice recruits have to study and rehearse in advance until it becomes an automatic, reflex action. And such decision making is not restricted to police training.

DELEGATION—A KEY WORD

Management expert, Peter Drucker, has been expounding these same basic concepts to the business community for decades. He also adds a note of warning about trivial decisions. Don't waste your time on decisions that others who work for you can and should be making. Save your mental energies for the major things. In other words, delegate.

Dwight L. Moody, the famous American evangelist at the turn of the century, once said he would rather put a thousand men to work than do the work of a thousand men.

Successfully fulfilling this task saves many frustrations. Delegating gets at the heart of directing a given group. Without delegation, a leader will be constantly enmeshed in a morass of secondary detail that can tear down and inhibit primary responsibilities. Someone has well said that a leader's value to the organization is measured not by what is on the desk but what passes over it.

WHAT NOT TO DELEGATE

One reason for delegation is to free the leader to perform certain key functions, which should never be turned over to others. They may be shared, but never completely delegated. Examples of this are: (1) setting objectives—for the division or department; (2) building teamwork—by organizing the work for maximizing coordination, communication and cooperation; (3) coaching and developing subordinates—to acquire knowledge and skill and to increase motivation and job satisfaction; (4) setting individual goals—on quantity, quality, costs and time.

In addition, disciplinary matters should never be delegated. Final authority in such matters always remains with the leader.

CHALLENGES IN CHRISTIAN DELEGATION

Managing volunteer workers presents several unique challenges. When you delegate part of your work to a volunteer, it is important to make sure: (1) you believe that the volunteer can do the job, (2) you have a clear understanding as to when each worker is going to report back to you, and (3) you have all the backup assistance each person may need. By carefully spelling out what is to be delegated, and by making sure the volunteer has both the time and the know-how to do the job, many problems can be avoided.

A second, and less obvious, problem in delegation results from that which is usually a major advantage of the Christian organization—its sense of common purpose and direction. Many subordinates believe they know what's best for the organization. Instead of seeing the task you have delegated to them as coming from you, they see it as part of the organization's task. With such a perception, their feedback and communication about what they are doing can easily break down. Again, this kind of problem can best be handled by clearly spelling out ahead of time what is to be done and what the checkpoints are along the way.

DECISION HELPERS

Interestingly, the most important decisions we make in life are often decided during our youthful years. The decision to accept Christ, the decision about education, the decision for our career and the decision to marry are often made before the ages of 22 or 23—long before we're fully aware of the consequences. That's unfortunate, but it's a fact of life.

To help people of all ages make better decisions, leaders need four kinds of people to provide support.

1. Look for a Barnabas—A "son of encouragement." Barnabas approached Saul of Tarsus when most other members of the Church still feared this former persecutor (see Acts 11:25). Barnabas remained as the encourager even after Saul (now called Paul) gained authority over him (see Acts 13:43).

2. Every leader needs a Timothy. Here is a fellow worker in the faith—a spiritual son—who also serves as a

loyal soldier for his commander (see Acts 16:1-3, Rom. 16:21, 1 Tim. 1:2, 18; 2 Tim. 2:3).

3. Christian decision makers need an Epaphroditus. "Yet I considered it necessary to send to you Epaphroditus, my brother, fellow worker, and fellow soldier" (Phil. 2:25). The Greek word *epaphroditos* connotes one who is "devoted to." Leaders need a devoted peer they can rely upon.

4. Every leader has to be accountable to a specific group of people. Whether it's an official board or a group of responsible Christians, somebody has to hold the leader's feet to the fire. We'll have a great deal more to say about this in our next chapter on responsibility.

WHY INDECISION?

According to a study of *un*successful executives in more than 200 firms, conducted by the Laboratory of Psychological Studies of the Stevens Institute of Technology, Hoboken, New Jersey, inability to make decisions is one of the principal reasons that administrators fail. In fact, this inability-to-make-decisions syndrome is a much more common reason for administrative failure than lack of specific knowledge or technical know-how.

Most human beings dislike making decisions. Indecision is generally more comfortable. All of us are conscious of the desire to put off deciding. But few of us are fully aware of the degree to which habitual inability to make decisions interferes with the realization of our full potential and the attainment of our goals in life. Psychiatrists have discovered that every one of us indulges in all kinds of unconscious devices to cover up our indecisiveness.

Procrastination—simply not getting around to doing things—is one such device. Others are swayed by circumstances or the temptation to leave decision making to someone else. Sometimes people cloud the issues to such a degree that they leave no basis upon which to make a decision.

Why are decisions so painful that we sometimes go to ridiculous lengths to avoid them? One reason is that any decision—large or small—involves the risk of being wrong. And being wrong in business could mean losing a job and/or seriously affecting the organization's future. Another reason is that every decision involves a judgment of goals and values. However, unless an individual has the courage to make choices and take risks, even when the stakes are high, that leader is not cut out for executive responsibility.

Some administrators await the views and reports of subordinates as a crutch to lean upon—someone else to blame. For others, the element of personal popularity enters into the decision-making process. The administrative "boss" may not wish to alienate colleagues or stand aloof from them.

Harry Truman was certainly correct in realizing "the buck stops here." The administrator must accept the fact that not every decision will be a popular one. Quoting Truman again, "If you can't stand the heat, stay out of the kitchen."

Several years ago the captain of a supertanker bound for London was sailing in the North Sea. It was winter, when storms on that body of water are unpredictable. Both the weather reports and the barometer predicted extremely heavy conditions. A veteran of many years at sea, the captain wondered if he should not put into a French port rather than attempt to make London. However, he delayed making his decision, hoping the storm would pass. By the time he realized his mistake, he was in such heavy seas that he no longer had a choice—the decision had been taken from his hands.

Failure to make up his mind resulted in one of the largest oil spills in fuel tanker history and the pollution of hundreds of miles of beaches on both sides of the English Channel. The cost ran into multiplied millions of dollars, both in loss from the spillage and from law suits. The

---

Learn from your mistakes and keep going. In fact, don't call them mistakes at all; call them education.

---

human factor, too, was costly: the captain's license was revoked and he, along with scores of others, needlessly spent weeks in court. All because one administrator couldn't make up his mind.

The means we use to deceive others and ourselves into thinking it is not yet time to face a major decision are myriad, but in many instances they can be recognized by telltale phrases that spring to the lips when the mind is not yet ready to make a commitment. Here are a few of them:

"I'm going to need a lot more time to think this one over."

"You can't rush into something like this overnight."

"I don't want to do anything that's going to upset the status quo."

"The time isn't ripe to go ahead."

"We ought to sit on this idea for awhile."

"I'm going to have to study the situation."

"Let's get a little more collective thinking on this."

"I'm going to wait until all the facts are in."

It is a curious paradox that sometimes these objections

are justifiable reasons for not making a decision at the moment. They are sensible stop-look-listen signs to prevent the catastrophes that might result from off-the-cuff, half-baked thinking. But more often than not, they are excuses, whose results can be catastrophic. Sleeping on a problem, for example, allows time for one's subconscious to contribute to a solution. But when an administrator turns a request of "let's sleep on it" into a Rip-van-Winkle hibernation, then it becomes an escape mechanism.

DON'T CALL IT A "MISTAKE"

Mistakes are valuable. The genius inventor Thomas Edison was one day faced by two dejected assistants, who told him, "We've completed our seven hundredth experiment and we still don't have an answer. We have failed."

"No, my friends," said Edison, "we haven't failed. We know more about this subject than anyone else alive. And we're closer to finding the answer, because now we know seven hundred things not to do." Edison went on to tell his colleagues, "Don't call it a mistake. Call it an education."

What a marvelous perspective. I don't know how many additional tries it took before Edison achieved success, but we all know that eventually he and his colleagues *did* see the light. Literally.

Learn from your mistakes and keep going. In fact, don't call them mistakes at all; call them *education*.

Ted Williams, one of the greatest baseball batters of all time, failed 6 times out of 10 in his best year when he batted .400! Babe Ruth is another example from baseball. He is remembered as the Home Run King, even though his home-run record has been broken in recent years by Henry Aaron. Of even greater interest, though, is the fact that for years Babe held the record for strikeouts. Yet few people remember his failures. Indeed, it *is* the percentage that counts.

I've always been encouraged by the words of Charles Kettering: "You will never stub your toe standing still. The faster you go, the more chance there is of stubbing your toe, but the more chance you have of getting somewhere." And, like the turtle, you really will go nowhere at all unless you stick your neck out. So it's back to our basic decision to *act*. To *do something*. I've heard psychologists say that action—any kind of action—is a tremendous cure for depression, even if it's no more than a walk around the block.

Franklin D. Roosevelt once said, "It is common sense to take a method and try it. If it fails, admit it frankly. But above all, *try something*." Go for it!

Many of the administrator's most important decisions are choices between different sets of values. Which should take priority over others and why? I like the way Professor David Moore of the Graduate School of Business Administration at Michigan State University put it in an address to students in the early 1970s:

> The administrator's loneliest hours are spent in choosing, not between right and wrong, but between two rights. His most creative moments are those in which he successfully integrates values, bringing diverse ideas together into new arrangements.[2]

FIVE STEPS TOWARD A PRECISION DECISION

Granted that decision making is an all-important administrative function and that choosing the right decision often spells the difference between success and failure, the next question that naturally arises is: How does one go about arriving at the best possible decision in a given situation at a given time? Try this list:

1. Identify the problem.
2. Put it down in the clearest language possible.
3. Examine it painstakingly. Get all the facts you can.
4. List the possible choices open to you and what each choice will lead to.
5. Then make your decision on the basis of the facts, scrutinized by the values in which you believe.

Let me give you an example. One of the greatest challenges I've ever had in my life was back in 1959 when I was scheduled to lead 40 American Christian leaders to a youth congress in Madras, South India. We were to leave the United States on December 27. On Christmas Eve I received word from Washington, D.C., that all of the visas in our passports had been canceled because we were thought to be a political organization. Several thousand delegates would be waiting for us in Madras, and here was the disturbing news that we could not enter the country.

As I prayed that Christmas Eve and asked the Lord to give me some assurance and guidance, my eyes fell on a phrase underlined in my New Testament from 1 John 3:20, "God is greater." I said to the Lord in my prayer, "Lord, here's a great opportunity to prove that you are greater than any government or any mountain to be climbed!"

I went to New York to meet with my colleagues the day after Christmas. There, we received our passports from Washington with the visa page canceled out. I indicated that I would refund their travel costs and they could go back home, or they could come along with me as far as Israel to see what would happen. All 40 said they wanted to move as far as possible toward the goal of getting to the congress in India.

As a leader, every decision you ever make will ultimately be the result of weighing two factors: advantages versus disadvantages.

I left a colleague back in Washington to wrestle with the embassy there and to be in constant contact with the Indian leadership in the capital city of New Delhi.

Meanwhile, our group went on to the Holy Land, as scheduled, for a few days. On New Year's Eve I received a transatlantic phone call from Washington. My colleague's opening word was simply, "Hallelujah." I knew then that God had answered our prayers.

The call indicated we should go to Beirut, Lebanon, the next day, New Year's Day. The Indian Embassy would be opened at 4:00 P.M., and the visas would be restamped into our passports. Two miracles: (1) No embassy in the world is open on New Year's Day—but they *did* open the Indian Embassy in Beirut! (2) Never is a visa, once canceled, restamped into the same passport. But they did so, for 40 of us! We arrived on time and enjoyed great blessing in the Madras Congress!

Care and persistence in applying this five-step method

to even minor decisions will increase your capacity to apply it to larger ones. Then eventually, when one of life's biggest decisions is thrust upon you, the time and effort you have learned to take in developing the faculty of making logical, objective decisions will have endued you with the skills and wisdom to make good decisions in the larger, more important matters.

PROS VERSUS CONS

As a leader, every decision you ever make will ultimately be the result of weighing two factors: advantages versus disadvantages. Except for the borderline elements that may not be clear gains or losses, this is exactly like making up a balance sheet. Instead of balancing figures, you balance advantages against disadvantages.

It is well to remember, however, that some benefits greatly outweigh corresponding disadvantages, and vice versa. The appropriate "weights" for each entry are not all equal. Be sure to weigh different factors according to their importance if you expect good decisions from the use of this method.

Benjamin Franklin, our wise American patriot, wrote a letter to Joseph Priestley in 1722 in which he had this to say about his personal decision-making procedures:

"My way is to divide half a sheet of paper by a line into two columns, writing at the top of one *Pro* and over the other *Con*. Then, after three or four days' consideration, I put down under the different headings, short hints of the different motives, that at different times occur to me, either for or against the measure at hand.

"When I have thus got them all together in one view, I endeavor to estimate their respective weights; and where I find two—one on each side that seem equal—I strike them both out. If I find a *Pro* reason that is equal to any two *Con* reasons, I strike out the three. If I judge some two *Con* reasons equal to three *Pro* reasons, I strike out the five. And thus proceeding, I find at length where the balance lies; and if, after a day or two of further consideration, nothing new that is of importance occurs on either side, I come to a determination accordingly.

"And, though the weight of reasons cannot be taken with the precision of algebraic quantities, yet, when each is thus considered, separately and comparatively, and the whole lies before me, I think I can judge better and am less liable to make a rash step; and in fact I have found great advantage from this kind of equation, in what may be called *moral* or *prudential algebra*."[3]

My mention of Benjamin Franklin's formula is not to suggest that all administrators must consciously plod through a long, detailed list before arriving at a decision. Undoubtedly, most administrators who have actually proven their outstanding capacity to make sound decisions, often at lightning speed, would say, "No, I never do anything like that! I simply get the important facts, estimate the situation, and decide."

Yet I am sure that if we could peer into the unconscious workings of their minds when they are in the throes of decision-making, we would find that many of the steps outlined above are regularly taken in preparing for that critical event when the decision is to be made.

DECISIONS AND HUMANISM

Up till now, we've talked about personal issues. Now let's turn to some of the social aspects you are already facing in your ministry. A key reason you need good decision-making power is the relentless advance of secular humanism. Secular humanism worships the use of human intellect by rejecting God and canonizing reason as supreme. Though perhaps less blatant than ancient gods of wood and stone, such idolotry is equally destructive.

Secular humanism has its roots in the eighteenth century "Enlightenment", which taught that man is the master of personal fate and captain of the soul. We see this heresy taking root in the educational system from preschool to post graduate institutions. But we often overlook its sinister shadow in other circles.

Here are some of the humanistic issues that will tax the decision-making ability of tomorrow's leaders. These are taken from an article by Donald Bloesch which appeared in *Eternity* magazine.

Secular Humanism

The ideology of welfare liberalism, which seeks to solve human problems through social engineering, is one manifestation of secular humanism. But the ideology of free enterprise capitalism (classical liberalism), which believes the free market contains the solution to the human malaise, is definitely another. Messianic socialism, with its dialectical materialism, is one of the more virulent fruits of secular humanism.

The Moral Majority, and other like-minded fundamentalist and evangelical groups, often concentrate unduly on the left-wing expressions of these issues. But if secular humanism is a wolf, then other wild dogs stalk the flock as well.

Nationalism

Easy to overlook is the threat of nationalism. This sentiment enthrones the values and traditions of the nation or *Volk* (people). It elevates the national or racial heritage over the autonomous individual—as in classical liberalism—or the political party—as in communism. While secular humanism subverts the family by endorsing sexual freedom, nationalism—though posing as the family's defender—subordinates it to the interests of the wider community, the nation-state, which is adorned with a kind of mystical aura.

American fundamentalism has been unable to perceive or appreciate this threat from the political right. This may account for fundamentalism's lack of credibility when it addresses issues that should command the attention of all people of moral sensitivity, including pornography, value-free sex education, and abortion.

Technological Materialism

We should also consider the decisions imposed by technological materialism, which Jacques Ellul has called the dominant ideology in the modern industrialized nations. According to this world-view and life-view, the prime virtues are utility, efficiency and productivity. People who make no visible contribution to the betterment of society, such as the aged, the retarded, and the severely handicapped, are pushed to one side or even regarded as expendable.

Whereas a great many secular humanists are inner-directed and stress personal integrity, technological materialists are other-directed, emphasizing loyalty to the organization, whether this be the state, corporation or union. While a significant number of secular humanists prize individuality and freedom, technological materialists encourage the dependence of humanity on technology.

Mysticism

A more subtle challenge to you as a Christian decision maker is mysticism—that perennial temptation to turn away from the pursuit of pleasure and power in search of that other world union with the Eternal. The growing penetration of Eastern religions into the industrial West has presented a new alternative for many. There are many forms of mysticism: some good, some less than helpful. We need to be aware of what form of mysticism we espouse.

Mysticism usually presents itself as a world-denying philosophy, but some neo-mystics actually stress immersion in the world, finding God in the depths of human existence. Whereas secular humanism celebrates the fulfillment of the self, mysticism emphasizes the loss of the self in the collective unconscious, the cosmic process or the undifferentiated unity.

Mysticism is especially prevalent among those in our churches and theological schools who are intent on recovering a lost, "bankrupt" spirituality. It is also found among certain radical feminists and New Age proponents. Wherever it rears its head, it's a force with which you need to reckon.

Nihilism

Perhaps most sinister of all is the mounting peril of nihilism—the denial of all norms and values. Nihilism is particularly fostered by the technological mentality, which elevates efficiency over ideology and religion. Technocrats try to give technology a rational direction, but the temptation is almost irresistible to sacrifice ends for means. Moreover, a technology without aim or purpose, a "soulless" technology, is more destructive than constructive. Indeed, the social agenda of nihilism is generally the overthrow of all existing social institutions and all norms. Nihilism ushers in the new barbarians, who are intent on destroying rather than creating, but they destroy in vain hope that something new and durable will result. The dramatic rise in international terrorism is a manifestation of the unleashing of the spirit of nihilism.

Nihilists, like occultists, are generally irrationalists, even as secular humanists and technological materialists are supreme rationalists. If the modern age is correctly characterized by what Francis Schaeffer calls "the flight from reason," it seems that nihilism, fascism, and nationalism may be greater threats than secular humanism. [4]

These complex issues of humanism and other challenges to you in Christian leadership may seem to be enough to make your head swim and your heart sink. At the same time, the decades ahead are filled with a sea of opportunity for you once you have gained the experience to make right decisions.

RIGHT DECISION REVIEW

1. Approach decision making with the same respect an officer holds for the use of deadly force.

2. Delegate often; delegate well.

3. Seek the help of your own personal Barnabas, Timothy, Epaphroditus and elders.

4. Beware indecision.

5. Look on mistakes as education.

6. Use the 5 steps for a "Precision Decision."

7. View the complexities of humanism as a reminder of how much you need good decision-making abilities and as a practice field for developing good decision-making

skills. There will be many more fields of equal challenge to test your skills as a leader.

Earlier I spoke of police academy training that prepares officers to get ready, aim and *make decision*. But we also learned about the Deadly Force Review Board to whom they must answer. Christian leadership has some of the same requirements. Perhaps now is a good time for you to unstrap your holster and join us in chapter 8 for a look at responsibility and accountability.

Chapter Eight

RESPONSIBILITY
and
ACCOUNTABILITY
The Price
of Leadership

*Real change and
emotional growth come
from facing our
weaknesses and
personality defects; by
taking seriously the
criticism leveled at us by
friends and foes alike.*

*"If you want something done,
put someone in charge
who really wants to make it work."*

Peter Drucker[1]

How real is the next century to you?

At a recent planning conference, Dr. David Mc-Kenna, president of Asbury Theological Seminary and author of the best-seller, *Megatruth*, related this story about the future. "We spent Thanksgiving with two of our grandchildren. I was brought into time perspective when one came forward with a T-shirt that read, 'Lansing Christian School, 1999, the Last Class of the 20th Century.' Not to be outdone, his little sister, two years younger, came out with her T-shirt, 'Lansing Christian School, 2001, a Space Odyssey.'"

That was several years ago. The next millennium is already in our midst through the lives of those who expect us to help provide what they need to survive. In that sense, we are responsible today for the outcome of tomorrow.

A SENSE OF URGENCY

I remember the sense of urgency and responsibility that drove us in those early days. At a World Congress in Berlin some years ago we had a population clock that was set at 4 billion people to be reached for Christ. The number is now 5 billion. We talked about the number of people being added every day to the world's population and felt a responsibility to reach them all.

We looked at the word *responsibility* and saw in it "the ability to respond." Two types of response seemed closest to the heart of God: individual worship and world evangelization. We felt the very names of God, from Jehovah to Creator, to Lord, to Master and Father, demanded worship. But not our worship alone. The names also demanded the worship of our brothers in all parts of the world.

We saw how often *world* was used in the New Testament. "God was in Christ reconciling the world to Himself" (2 Cor. 5:19). "For God so loved the world that He gave His only begotten Son" (John 3:16). "Go into all the world and preach the gospel" (Mark 16:15). "You shall be witnesses to Me in Jerusalem, and in all Judea and Samaria, and to the end of the earth" (Acts 1:8). How could we worship God as a lone parishioner and not respond to His concern for the rest of the world's congregation?

World evangelization, above everything else, marked those post-war years. We didn't seek a large church and congregation nor a magnificent ministry. We didn't seek a personal organization. What we did seek was to reach the world with the gospel of Christ, His church, His ministry and His organization. And we made a great deal of progress in those days.

But so much still remains to be done today and in the years ahead of us. My agenda has not changed. I'm still committed to world evangelism, the family and to encouraging others to live their lives with commitment and responsibility.

That's why, in my own way, I want to pass on this torch of leadership to you, in full belief that you will keep the flame of leadership alive.

So far in this book we've seen the importance of commitment, goal setting, motivation, enthusiasm, honesty, courage and decision making for successful leadership. These traits take on even greater significance as we explore the importance of responsibility, priorities and the future.

My dream for you is that this information will help you discover what unique talents and God-given gifts you have to offer, and that you'll develop these gifts to their greatest potential, to the service of Christ.

Like the apostle Paul, who held such a profound interest in those he was training for new leadership responsibilities, "I beseech you therefore, brethren, by the mercies of God, that you present your bodies a living sacrifice, holy, acceptable to God, *which is* your reasonable service" (Rom. 12:1). And that's my prayer for you.

THE 2/4/6 CLUB

Many years ago I heard a friend of mine, Pastor Ray Stedman, talk about a special group of men he had gathered to meet with him on a weekly basis. These men were not all members of his congregation, but were close friends who held each other accountable in their spiritual walk. He said his experience with those men was one of the most meaningful experiences in his life.

After thinking about it, and realizing the need for such accountability in my own life, I talked to my pastor about it. Dr. Ray Ortlund expressed similar deep needs and feelings, so we met a couple of times to discuss the concept. Then we invited several men to meet with us. Some of the original group dropped out, but ultimately there were six of us who met together for more than 10 years in a local restaurant. We called it the 2/4/6 Club, indicating that there were six of us, who met on the second and fourth Friday mornings of each month for breakfast. We met at 7:00 A.M. for approximately an hour and a half.

It was not a prayer group; although we did pray together. It was not a Bible study group; although we did spend time in the Word. It was a time of meeting and growing together, appreciating each other and sharing our individual spiritual pilgrimages. There was no appointed leader and no agenda. We met to share experiences, to laugh, to weep. We rejoiced in our successes. We also shared and wept together over our failures.

Those meetings proved to be a tremendously significant experience in my life. The constituency of the group has changed now, and I meet with another group on a monthly basis, but not quite in the same depth as the earlier group.

During one of our times together, we decided each of us needed to develop a strategy for spiritual effectiveness. We agreed that in the month following we would each develop such a strategy and share it with the group. Though that happened nearly 20 years ago, I still carry in my wallet what has become a tattered yellow card. The heading reads: "A Spiritual Strategy for Maximum Spiritual Effectiveness." Over the years I have reviewed the list frequently and tried to keep my feet to the fire regarding the following six challenges:

Strategy for Maximum Spiritual Effectiveness

1. I deliberately place myself daily before God to allow Him to use me as He wills (see Rom. 12:1,2).
2. Ask God at a specific time *daily* to reveal His strategy and will for me that day.
3. Set and achieve a goal for personal spiritual development through reading one significant book per week.
4. Isolate a known point of weakness (spiritually), and work on it with the help of the Holy Spirit to correct and improve this weakness.
5. Make a study of several Bible people who are good examples—and seek deliberately to emulate them in their strong points.
6. Set up a measuring device to check spiritual development (quantitatively) and measure regularly.

These six points have helped me immensely. But they would have been little more than ink on paper had it not been for the sense of responsibility and accountability I shared with the 2/4/6 Club.

FACETS OF RESPONSIBILITY

Responsibility is a jewel with many facets. First, as Christian leaders we are responsible to God. Some day, we must all answer for our own actions. That sobering reality makes me extremely grateful for mercy and forgiveness. Second, we are responsible to our closest loved ones, friends and relatives. Any decision that is truly good for the well-being of the organization will also be good for that of our family and friends. Third, we are responsible to the board of the church or ministry involved. And fourth, to the people we lead.

Often it was the people who criticized me the most who helped me the most.

In living up to these responsibilities, we dare not settle for the status quo. Two words not in God's vocabulary are *mediocrity* and *average*. There is nothing average about God. There's nothing mediocre about spiritual matters. And there must be nothing mediocre about our leadership!

PAYING THE PRICE

Leadership is the sum total of many emotional accounts, all of which must be kept in balance. These accounts include everything from representing the entire group to living in personal loneliness; from mental strain to physical fatigue. But the price that takes its greatest toll on most leaders is one that closely relates to accountability. And that is criticism.

Often it was the people who criticized me the most who helped me the most. It was tough to accept it at the time, but how wonderfully redemptive such situations became! The same can be true for you. The only way you really get to know yourself is by getting honest feedback from others. Otherwise we will never know how we come across to people.

Backslappers help us feel better about ourselves, but

we seldom profit by their enthusiasm. Real change and emotional growth come when we face our weaknesses and personality defects and take seriously the criticism leveled at us by friends and foes alike.

Undeserved criticism is equally beneficial. Through it we discover misconceptions and communication problems that may need improvement.

HOT BLAME AND WARM APPRECIATION

A number of years ago, football's coaching great, Paul "Bear" Bryant was quoted as saying this about taking criticism and taking praise.

> I'm just a plowhand from Arkansas, but I have learned how to hold a team together. How to lift some men up, how to calm down others, until finally they've got one heartbeat together, a team. There's just three things I'd ever say:
> If anything goes bad, I did it.
> If anything goes semi-good, then we did it.
> If anything goes real good, then you did it.
> That's all it takes to get people to win football games for you.

Write this down where you can see it every day: *There's no end to what you can accomplish if you don't care who gets the credit.*

AN IMPERFECT SCIENCE

Unfortunately leadership terminology is not precise. Words like *responsibility, measurement, controls, feedback, audit,* and *accountability* are frequently used interchangeably. Joe Batten defines control as "information provided to measure the performance of men, money, materials, time, and space in achieving predetermined objectives." I'm grateful to my friend, Frank Goble, author of *Excellence in Leadership* for many of the examples that follow.

Accountability is a closely related word but it implies more. Perhaps the simplest explanation is that people in an organization are given responsibility for a task and then are held accountable for its accomplishment. Controls are various methods of measuring accountability. Accountability implies measurement of results. It also implies, and this is the important distinguishing feature, that some other individual or group of individuals is observing the measurement. When a leader is held accountable for something, there is no passing the buck.

Edward Glaser, a West Coast consulting psychologist, offers an example of how accountability motivates executives. One of his client firms had a manufacturing division that was doing poorly. Operating costs were high, but productivity was low and the division was losing money. On Glaser's first visit he found a typical pattern of buck passing. When he talked to the department heads, each placed the blame on others.

Glaser recommended to the corporation president that the name of the game be changed from "surviving by not admitting any mistakes" to "frankly admitting problems and solving them or perishing." In executive conference, goals were established regarding the percentage of the market this division should expect to capture if design, price, quality and service were first-rate. Then department heads were told that unless they could capture the desired share of the market, the company would stop making that product and lay off the 60 or so hourly workers involved.

Once it became clear that they would be held account-able for specific results, the supervisors shifted, with the help of the consultant, to a problem-solving approach. Three months after the change in approach, productivity had risen 32 percent, and rejections had dropped from 12 percent to 9 percent. In less than three years after inter-vention, productivity was 190 percent greater than in the beginning, and rejects had dropped to only 3.2 percent.

When accountability is used in a positive manner to establish the basis for approval, recognition, achievement and promotion, the results tend to be positive.

There are many devices to establish accountability—performance reviews, audits, inspection reports, and the like. Executives need to be careful what they measure, especially if measurement is coupled with pay and advancement. When a school principal established attend-ance at meetings as one of his criteria for teacher perform-ance, teachers made it a point to attend meetings. Unfor-tunately this activity had virtually no correlation with their major objective, which was to be effective classroom teachers. In most cases measurement of an activity will cause an increase in people's productivity even though the measurement is not related to pay or promotion.

When accountability is used in a positive manner to establish the basis for approval, recognition, achievement and promotion, the results tend to be positive. When man-agement uses statistical information in a critical and destructive way, the employees react accordingly and may even attempt to conceal their errors and falsify records.[2]

POSITIVE VERSUS NEGATIVE ACCOUNTABILITY

Peter Drucker gives two examples showing the difference between positive and negative accountability, which he says "will inflict incalculable harm by demoralizing management, and by seriously lowering the effectiveness of managers." He cites General Electric as an example for the positive approach.

General Electric has a special control service—the traveling auditors. The auditors study every one of the managerial units of the company thoroughly at least once a year. But their report goes to the manager of the unit studied. There can be little doubt that the feeling of confidence and trust in the company, which even casual contact with General Electric managers reveals, is directly traceable to this practice of using information for self-control rather than for control from above.[3]

But the General Electric practice is by no means common or generally understood. Typical management thinking is much closer to the practice exemplified by a large chemicals company.

In this company a control section audits all managerial units of the company. Results of the audits do not go, however, to the managers audited. They go only to the president, who then calls in the managers to confront them with the audit of their operations. What this has done to morale is shown in the nickname the company's managers have given the control section: "the president's Gestapo." Indeed, more and more managers are now running their units not to obtain the best performance but to obtain the best showing on the control-section audits.[4]

We've all felt the sting of misdirected accountability audits. We cannot control how other people treat us, but we can control how we treat other people and how we react to the treatment we receive from others.

FACE TO FACE WITH RESPONSIBILITY

The story is told of a trusted adviser of President Lincoln who recommended a candidate for the Lincoln cabinet. Lincoln declined, and when he was asked why, he said, "I don't like the man's face."

"But the poor man is not responsible for his face," his adviser insisted.

"Every man over forty is responsible for his face," Lincoln replied, and the prospect was considered no more.

ACCOUNTABILITY TOWARD GOD AND MAN

How can we then as leaders balance our responsibility toward the earthly needs of our neighbors without neglecting the loftier principles of God?

The perfect model for this is the person of our Lord Jesus Christ. Jesus commanded and carried on both kinds of ministry. He met spiritual needs and he met physical needs determined by the immediate condition. In John 3 Jesus spoke to Nicodemus about being born again. And we, rightly, must place a strong emphasis upon such an experience.

But Jesus also addressed Himself frequently to the matter of caring about people who were hurting physically, emotionally and socially. He sought to minister to the whole person.

To my way of thinking, this is the essence of true Christian leadership. It's a principle of accountability we can practice on our back doorstep and on the other side of the world.

We have the example of the apostle Paul who once sent Titus and two other outstanding church leaders to deliver the relief of material gifts (see 2 Cor. 8:16-24). Here is recorded in one instance in Scripture three significant individuals who left, at least temporarily, their evangelism work and went to help Christians in deep physical need in Jerusalem. Paul himself did this twice (see Acts 11:27, Rom. 15:25). He left his evangelistic and missionary efforts to meet social concern situations.

The whole being of the individual is extremely important. I don't believe we can separate or dichotomize the two aspects of what we call evangelism on the one hand and having a social concern and social involvement on the other.

I don't choose to equate what we used to call the social gospel with social action or social concern. There is a marked difference, and Jesus is, as always, the perfect model with His holistic approach to the human being. As Christians, we must recognize the dignity of the individual and know that God loves the person in the African bush, the sophisticate in Rio de Janiero, and the reader of this book—and everyone in between. And we must accept the responsibility that we cannot preach sermons and expect to get results to people who are dying of hunger or who are in famine situations. First of all, we must feed them and win the right to be heard—whether it's the refugee across the equator or the derelict across town.

Let me illustrate this truth by World Vision's work in Ethiopia. Long before this country became the focus of world attention, we were already working among many of the nomadic tribes in the southern part of that impoverished nation. These people have suffered tremendous famine and many thousands of them, particularly children, have died of starvation. World Vision has had the privilege of ministering to these people by feeding them, helping them with their crops, supplying seed and oxen, and training them in agricultural techniques. As a direct result, we have been able, with the assistance of national church leaders in Ethiopia, to effectively preach the gospel and assist in the building of a number of chapels.

ALL NATIONS MUST GO

In 1968, I had the privilege of attending the Asia-South Pacific Congress on Evangelism in Singapore. I was one of some 70 men and women from the West who were observers at the Congress. Eleven hundred delegates from 25 Asian nations met daily. The delegates were evangelists, heads of denominational groups in Asia, key pastors and leaders in the Church. They came at the invitation of the Billy Graham Evangelistic Association, which was largely the sponsoring agency for the Congress.

After a few days of the Congress sessions, I noticed a dramatic and drastic change in the attitude of the men and women who were present. There seemed to be a growing realization that the Great Commission set forth in Matthew 28 was given not only to the church in the West—in Europe and in the United States—but to the church, everywhere. It was every believer's responsibility.

A holy excitement came over that group of 1100 leaders when they began to strategize together as to how they could be involved in sending the gospel, as well as in receiving its message. It was a great moment!

For so long the problem with these receiving churches was that they had been conditioned to the syndrome of accepting and assimilating the message from the West and using it by contextualizing it in their own nations. Good enough, as far as it went. But they had neglected to see that the Great Commission was given to every believer, every church congregation and every nation. And, in strategizing together the last half dozen days of that Congress, they began to lay plans whereby the dynamic church in Korea, for example, could begin sending out missionaries across Asia. It's thrilling to note that since that time the Korean church has sent missionaries into Africa and Latin America as well. In addition, several hundred Korean missionaries have followed the Korean influx to Europe.

Strikingly, the same thing happened with the leadership of the church in Japan. They have, since that time, had an effective strategy for sending missionaries out to Brazil, where there are hundreds of thousands of Japanese living in its cities.

The whole impact of that Congress was overwhelming. Those leaders accepted the responsibility of world evangelism as being *their* task, as well as that of those who had been sending the gospel to them for many years. In that sense all nations are accountable to "all nations."

ANOTHER PIECE OF THE PUZZLE

Like every personal skill we've covered, this review of accountability and responsibility is designed to help encourage you to prepare for the decades ahead. The needs of tomorrow are much like a jigsaw puzzle. Each piece of itself is a meaningless blur. But the more parts you assemble, the more the picture emerges and the more you see the importance of each individual piece.

Let's reach into the stack of scattered pieces and examine another important aspect of the twenty-first century—one which challenges all of us to become more responsible leaders.

THE NEW WAVE OF PENTECOSTALS AND CHARISMATICS

Christianity is subject to the ebb and flow of many streams of thought. Understanding the latest philosophical tides in the Church will help us render more effective service to those believers who turn to us for leadership.

In 1975 there were 61 million Pentecostals and charismatics worldwide. Ten years later that number had nearly tripled to 169 million. It may be closer to 200 million, if we knew how to count China properly. The fastest growing church segment in America today is the independent charismatic churches, with more than 80,000 congregations, most of which have started since 1980.

This growth comes in the face of a steady decline for traditional denominations. In 1920 the seven mainline denominations accounted for 76 percent of American Protestants. Today they number barely half. Since the mid-'60s the mainliners have collectively lost more than 4,778,000 members. This prompted the Reverend Jerry Falwell's monthly magazine to say that "The Mainline is Becoming the Sideline."[5]

HIGH-OCTANE GOSPEL

"It's like gasoline," says evangelical historian George Marsden of Duke University Divinity School. "Once you discover all gasoline is the same, brand loyalty disappears, and any station will do. Only octane matters, and the mainline Protestant churches do not sell high-octane religion."[6]

High octane performance is one of the hallmarks of

Pentecostals and charismatics. But should it be their sole domain? C. Peter Wagner offers a challenging perspective in the International Bulletin of Missionary Research:

> When Jesus sent out his disciples he said, "Preach, saying, 'The kingdom of heaven is at hand.' Heal the sick, cleanse the lepers, raise the dead, cast out demons" (Matt. 10:7,8). When he gave the Great Commission he told his apostles to wait in Jerusalem until they were endued with power from on high (Luke 24:49). Power to heal the sick and cast out demons is a formidable asset in communicating the gospel cross-culturally.
>
> I am not suggesting that we all become Pentecostal or charismatic. I am neither myself. Yet for four years we have been teaching courses on this at Fuller Theological Seminary and have discovered that God is more than willing to give the rest of us the same power of the Holy Spirit that the Pentecostals and the charismatics have enjoyed for years. Many of us have not been open to it, however, largely because of the pervasive influence of secular humanism on Anglo-American culture. This same secular humanism has not influenced many ethnics nearly as much. The world of the supernatural with demons and angels, visions and dreams, is much more real to them than to many of us. Part of our kingdom ministry to them, as I see it, is to allow the power of God to be demonstrated among them in supernatural ways, not for the sake of being spectacular, but because it

is a New Testament way of encouraging the message of the gospel to be heard and accepted."[7]

At the start of this chapter we met a youngster who already owns a T-shirt with a reference to her class of 2001. Whether or not we understand the finer points of charismatics and Pentecostals; whether or not we know how to balance the needs of suffering humans with the perfect Word of God; whether or not we understand all the management principles of responsibility; we're accountable today for the face of tomorrow. The more we delve into these subjects and demonstrate our willingness to act on them, the more we can contribute. What are you saying to a child of the twenty-first century? The words don't really matter as long as your actions prove you believe the questions are part of your own personal responsibility.

RESPONSIBILITY REVISITED

1. Stay accountable with your own 2/4/6 Club.
2. Understand and apply the four facets of responsibility—God, family, superiors and followers.
3. Use accountability audits as an arm-on-the-shoulder and not a club-on-the-head.
4. Understand your responsibility toward the spiritual needs of the world at large.
5. Make it your responsibility to act on the needs created by new trends in the church.

Understanding the positive forces motivating effective leaders, we are now ready to look at those times when responsible leaders should *not* lead. We're ready to explore the perils of priority, the topic of chapter 9.

Chapter Nine

PRIORITIES
When Did You Leave Your Family?

Pastors, when on a
vacation, shouldn't
preach! They should
provide for a change of
pace by doing things that
are not part of their regular
routine. It is vital to give
the mind and body a chance
to regroup and recharge
itself.

*"The time is always right
to do what is right."*
Martin Luther King, Jr.[1]

We've examined how to be an effective leader through commitment and goal setting. We've explored the importance of motivation, enthusiasm, honesty and courage. We've learned how to make decisions and bear the responsibility for their outcome. All that remains now is to understand when *not* to apply these principles.

Ironically, one of the last dangers you encounter as an effective leader is the peril of becoming too involved—too committed to the task at hand rather than the duties at heart. Once you've proven to others how well the organization gets along *with* your leadership, you must then prove to yourself and your family how well it gets along *without* your leadership.

What good is a leader who steers the organization toward success but runs over friends and loved ones in the process? What good is a leader who propels the group to new heights of achievement and leaves the family behind? These possibilities are all too real. That's why every arriving leader needs to consider the question, When did you *leave* your family?

Not long ago the pastor of a large Los Angeles area church was interviewing men for his staff. He asked when they would like to take a day off during the week. He got several different replies: "Oh, it doesn't really matter." "I never take a day off." "I don't really need any time off." The pastor hired none of them.

Then he interviewed another young prospect. "What day of the week would you like off?"

"Well, I surely don't want Monday off. After the Sunday crunch, I'm in no shape to enjoy the next day. Let me have Thursday off. That's the best day of the week for me." That young man was hired.

Many ministers work 12 to 15 hours a day, and some rarely take a day off. What is so meritorious about working seven days a week and never taking off any time to rest and be with your family? God condemned the pagans of old for sacrificing their children on what they considered a religious altar. Does He feel any different about us today?

MARIJUANA LOW

It was a cold, rainy night. My son Gordon, then 21 years old, finally came home around 1:00 A.M., after a long night of smoking marijuana with his friends. I was livid, embarrassed, distraught and afraid. How could this young man whom we loved so much do this to his mother and me? It wasn't fair; it wasn't right. It was happening to other parents, but who would have ever thought it would have reared its ugly head in the Engstrom family?

We couldn't understand why. But this particular evening I held my peace, even though I had a mind to give Gordon a tongue lashing he'd never forget. I listened to him as he shouted that most Christians were phonies, the church was filled with hypocrites, and there were at least a hundred ways to God. And on and on he went.

The more I listened, the more something began to happen inside me. After a while, I no longer saw a son whose head was clouded from the effects of pot. Instead, I began to hear him. Even though I didn't—and don't— approve of anyone's ingesting drugs for recreational purposes, I knew that much of what Gordon had to say was true. The distance between us was real.

I can remember a hot tear falling on my cheek, then another and another as Gordon spoke. I knew in my heart he was also talking about me. I only tell you this story to say that although that winter evening in January 1968 was difficult, humiliating and upsetting, I think it may have been the first night I really listened to my son. In a fresh, new way, I was establishing a real relationship with Gordon—one that had been sacrificed in my rush to serve the families of other people. In serving others, I had left my own family behind. And now I was going back to meet this one beautiful and important member.

When did you leave your family?

HELP UNMEET

Bill Edwards was 38 years old. He had a pretty wife, two beautiful children, and was considered one of the outstanding pastors in the city. Bill and June were married while Bill was still in seminary. Their first child was born during his senior year. June never completed her college education but took a job to help Bill through seminary. Bill became an effective preacher and was greatly respected by both his assistant and the congregation. He worked hard on his sermons for a growing congregation. But because of a misplaced priority, Bill's wife left him at the height of his career.

Why? What went wrong?

Of all the human relationships described in the Bible, the highest and most significant is the one found in marriage. The apostle Paul could only compare it to the relationship of Christ and His church (see Eph. 5:22-33).

The most important decisions a person makes in life are: first, the decision to accept Christ as a spiritual mate, and second, the decision to accept another human being as a physical mate.

The disruption of this relationship creates tremendous spiritual repercussions. Peter tells us troubles in the relationship can even interfere with our prayers (see 1 Pet. 3:7).

If you're married, is your ministry as a leader built upon the foundation of a strong marriage relationship, or does your work move forward in spite of your relationship with your spouse?

You may respond in your own defense, "But this is the work God has called me to! My spouse understands that. That's one of the sacrifices we are making together."

Perhaps. But perhaps that is *your* view of the situation, and although it may be outwardly shared by your mate, inwardly—consciously or unconsciously—your loved one may feel quite differently.

I think two of the most important decisions a person makes in life are: first, the decision to accept Christ as a spiritual mate, and second, the decision to accept another human being as a physical mate. Here is something to be prayed through to make sure this is what you want to live with. I have seen so many leaders who have been irreparably hurt because they didn't have a mate who was supporting them. I have seen couples, each with his or her own personal agenda and ambitions. They were not a team. Each was pulling in different directions.

The teamwork of a husband and wife in the ministry is terribly important. This is not to say, for example, that a man and wife should have a comparable prominence in the public setting. But each needs to be fully supportive of the other. The most successful leaders I have seen are those who had good, solid, successful marriages, whether it's a Billy Graham or Cliff Barrows. And I've seen others who have struggled. One of Satan's most effective traps is to bring discord to a marriage. But the emergence of this problem only underscores the need for those who serve the bride of Christ to respect, love and cherish the one they have married.

HOMEBOUND SABBATICAL

I'm impressed by the example of my friend, James Dobson, founder of Focus on the Family. At one point in his career, Jim took seven years off with no speaking engagements in order to spend time with his daughter, who is now in college, and his son, now in high school; he wanted to be home with his family. Recently the seven years came to an end and now he's gradually beginning to appear in public rallies. Dr. Dobson saw the need in his life and met it. That's a rare insight today.

NEW DIRECTIONS

Ever since World War II, we've seen a sustained effort to diminish the importance of morals and family relationships. But this new morality is not new—it's older than Noah's ark—and it is not moral—it's contrary to everything that perpetuates a stable society. Leaders who face the twenty-first century still need the value system and priority structure that has proven itself for centuries.

I confess, my family life is not what I enjoyed as a youngster growing up. Even when we started raising our family, it was much different. For example, the day of the family devotion is almost past. Dorothy and I have only recently, in the last several years, resurrected our devotional life *together*. We've had our own personal devotions, but once again we're reading and praying together.

In this American Christian society we seldom talk together as families. We have different meal hours and we eat sitting in front of the television set. Many parents are so preoccupied with their favorite TV show they don't tuck their kids into bed anymore. And what ever happened to *family* vacations?

Even the church divides the family. Rarely do you see everyone sitting together in the church service. There's a junior church, senior night, Sunday School and nursery school. Then we try to patch it all back together with an occasional "family night."

FIRST THINGS FIRST

How do you sort it all out? Where do your Christian priorities lie? How does one find a balance between commitment to the Lord and the family? We can answer these questions by first understanding the meaning of priority.

Some view priority in terms of putting one thing before something else. Others may think of ranking items.

Priorities have both a when and an if. All priority questions are first about *when?"* We are faced with whether we are going to do an activity first, second, third, or perhaps never. By assigning such time ratings to events, we essentially put them in terms of priorities—what we are going to do when.

This comes from our need to choose the future over the past. Priorities should be determined by what lies ahead rather than what lies behind. Over the Archives Building in Washington, D.C., is the Shakespearean phrase *What Is Past Is Prologue.* This says it well.

Here is a list of questions you might want to consider in establishing priorities:

1. How urgent is it? When must it be done? Does it have to be done right now, today, soon or someday? When you ask this question, you may discover that something doesn't have to be done at all!

2. How important is it? Very important? Quite important? Somewhat important? Not so important? Note there is always a tension between the important and the urgent. But it is the urgent things that keep getting in the way of the important things, is it not? We covered the distinction between these two masqueraders in chapter 2. We are always faced with those things that have to be done "right now." The urgent often turns out to be the enemy of the important.

3. How often must it be done? Is it something that's done every day? Only occasionally? Or just sometimes? This will give us some insight as to how dependent we are on this event's occurrence.

4. Can someone else or some other organization do it

just as well? The answer might be no, perhaps, or yes. If the answer is yes, perhaps we should not be involved at all, but should turn the idea and suggestion over to some other committee, department or organization.

5. Is it part of a larger task to which we are committed? Very often we can get involved in goals that are attractive for the moment, but that really have nothing to do with our organization. This is probably the most subtle trap of all. How easy it is to get involved in interesting projects that really do not relate to where we hope our ministry is moving!

6. What will happen if it's not done at all? What will happen if we abandon this whole goal? Disaster? Trouble? Difficulty? Nothing? If nothing will happen, perhaps we have a clue that we shouldn't be involved in it in the first place.

7. Is this the best way? There will always be alternatives. But after we have decided upon one, we need to ask this final question.

There are many priority questions for you as a leader. For the Christian organization there is the question of which purpose—of all the possible ministries with which we could become involved—is the one God wants for *our* organization? Once we become involved in a ministry, we face the question of a choice between goals. Thus, of all the things that we could do to carry out the ministry, which seem most important to us now? Which should be postponed? Which should be abandoned? We can also think of priorities in terms of allegiance. What claims the highest priority in our lives?

The primary question should always be: Will this bring glory to God? Then we need to consider:

1. We can't minister to everyone. To whom do we want to minister?
2. We can't do everything. What must we do first?
3. We can't be everything. What is most important to me at this time?

Because both needs and situations change, these questions must be asked again and again. The cycle continues. We will face new problems and receive new information about the world in which we are working. Thus, we need to review our priorities continually.

POSTERIORITIES

You have undoubtedly already learned that organizations have a tremendous amount of natural inertia. Once individuals have been assigned to a task, and suborganizations such as boards or committees or departments have been formed, the groups tend to generate lives of their own. It is easy to stop asking, What is the goal of the Christian Education Committee this year? and start wondering, What should we do this year?

What we all need are *posteriorities*, statements of things that we are *not* going to do this year. Picture an organization as an alligator— it has a great tendency to grow a very large tail. Periodically someone needs to chop off the tail, so the alligator can keep moving! Perhaps we need a committee to decide each year which 10 percent of all the things we did last year we are *not* going to do again this year.

With this understanding of the process, I'd like to recommend these priorities for serving the family of God and man:

1. God first
2. Family second
3. Fellow Christians third
4. Work of Christ fourth.

WORKAHOLISM

One of the devil's favorite elixirs for blurring priorities and dissolving family unity is workaholism—especially in the Church. Studies today cite that members of the clergy occupy one of the most stressful positions in the American labor force.

As a pastor you may be convinced you are married to the church. But let me bring you in on a little secret: the church is already married. That's what the Bible says. In the New Testament the church is pictured as the Bride of Christ.

The minister must heed the instruction of Scripture. "But if any provide not for his own, and specially for those of his own house, he hath denied the faith, and is worse than an infidel" (1 Tim. 5:8, *KJV*). There is no exemption from family obligations and responsibilities.

Such a provision indeed may include much more than physical or financial support. If the pastor is overworked, why not reset priorities and share with the congregation the decision to place the family above the church? People in the pews will accept the pastor even more readily for this humanness. They face the same problem and will appreciate this example of guidance and courage.

Pastors, when on a vacation, shouldn't preach! They should provide for a change of pace by doing things that are not part of their regular routine. It is vital to give the mind and body a chance to regroup and recharge itself.

Many pastors, without necessarily intending to do so, convey the view by their own work habits, or by preaching, that church work must always have the highest priority in the lives of everyone. If not, people are often made to feel guilty because they have a split commitment. The message comes through, "Ye cannot serve God and mammon." This obviously is true, but the truth gets garbled through misinterpretation and false priorities.

Balance is one of the basic keys the workaholic needs to restore.

One family was seldom seen in the evening service at church. On several occasions the pastor heard family members being put down indirectly with such remarks as, "My, Bob and Jane, we missed you last Sunday night." Little did people realize that this wise pastor had given counsel to the family. Bob traveled a great deal during the week on his job. As a result he saw very little of his family.

One day, feeling guilty, he stopped by the pastor's study. "Pastor, I know I should come to the evening services, but I feel the need to be with my family on Sunday evenings."

The pastor wisely advised him to stay home. "Bob," said the minister, "stay home as long as you use the time to be with your family." That minister had rightly resolved the issue without creating any guilt for his layman friend.

Dr. C. Peter Wagner, associate professor of Latin American affairs at Fuller Theological Seminary School of World Mission in Pasadena, California, confessed in a published magazine article to being a converted workaholic. He says that some time ago he had an excruciating headache that lasted for 70 days and 69 nights. He sought spiritual counsel and looked to the Bible for help. He related the following:

> During the ordeal I was under excellent medical treatment. I put myself under the care of a highly competent chiropractor, consulting also with a medical doctor to be sure I was not missing any better option. The chiropractor studied a series of X-rays and used a combination of unintelligible polysyllables to describe what was wrong with my muscles, bones and nerves. Three or four visits per week to his clinic, exercise and diets eventually corrected certain structural defects. But my problem went deeper.[2]

After much soul-searching and spiritual examination, Wagner came to the conclusion that his problem was really very simple. He had been working too hard!

He continued:

> Simple? Who ever heard of God punishing someone for working too hard? I was always taught that work was a virtue. Would God be angry with someone who gave too much to the poor?[3]

Wagner resolved such questions in his mind and came to realize, before it was too late, that there is a price one pays when the addiction to work sets in. He was one of the fortunate ones. Today the term *workaholic* is a daily vocabulary word to him.

Wagner goes on in the article to show how he had

fallen into the typical trap of most workaholics, the praise that goes along with hard work. The usual pattern, he confessed, was hearing people comment, "I don't see how you possibly get done all that you do." That, he says, is the supreme pat on the back for the workaholic, and since such a person craves to hear it as a reward, the workaholic will work all the harder to get it. Wagner confessed this pride in productivity.

> Wasn't I proud of propelling myself out of bed and into high gear at 4:30 every morning? Wasn't I proud that while my neighbors were sleeping at 5:00 A.M. (imagine!) I was out in the street running a mile? Wasn't I proud of the number of books and articles I could get published in a year? Wasn't I proud of my ability to bring work home and continue through the evening with only a brief interruption for dinner? Wasn't I proud of foregoing vacations year after year so that I could produce more? Wasn't I proud of the number of miles I could travel and speaking engagements I could handle without a break? Wasn't I proud of dictating fat envelopes of belts on airplanes and shipping them home to my secretary? Wasn't I proud that when I would land in some exotic country I would invariably choose to work rather than take in the tourist attractions?
>
> Without the headache, I never would have realized what harmful effects this was having on me. I had developed strong guilt feelings about doing anything that would interrupt work. I could not stay in bed more than six hours, would not watch television, could not plan days

off or weekends without productive work, and
felt uncomfortable when I would go for a drive
with the family. I envied some of my friends
who could function on only four hours of sleep.
But even worse, I found myself judging others
for spending their time in such unproductive
ways. Imagine, watching the movie on an airplane rather than dictating letters! Through it
all, of course, I easily rationalized it as "serving
God," a simple process for a clergyman, but
handy also for almost any Christian workaholic. [4]

One of the most important words in our English language is *balance*. Extremes or tangents in any area of our
lives may well create confusion and distress. Balance is
one of the basic keys the workaholic needs to restore. In
the Gospel of Luke, the Apostle, commenting about Jesus'
childhood, wrote, "And Jesus increased in wisdom and
stature, and in favour with God and man" (Luke 2:52,
KJV).

Notice that Jesus dedicated His first years to living a
healthy, balanced life. Physically, intellectually, emotionally
and spiritually there was growth because all levels of His
life were integrated, thus, balanced. He combined all the
basic elements needed for a disciplined and well-rounded
life. He wants to do the same for us. Dr. John R.W. Stott
states it plainly in his book, *Balanced Christianity*: "It
seems that there is almost no pasttime the devil enjoys
more than tipping Christians off balance." [5]

SERVE THE FAMILY BY
SERVING YOURSELF

Workaholism is only one way to leave a family behind.

Over and above the obvious tragedy of divorce, there are many other ways for a leader to turn away from the followers.

Most of these estrangements trace back to one familiar cause, self-neglect. People are not a consumable product; they are a renewable resource. But all too often we act as if we could spend our entire life breathing out power without ever stopping to inhale strength.

What kind of strength does a leader need?

Recreation is one strength we need. We get so busy that we don't take time for physical exercise. For me it's golf. For others it may be tennis. Others enjoy jogging. I think these are scriptural. Paul talks about fitness in running and racing. We know our bodies are the temple of the Holy Spirit. What kind of structure can a leader build with weak materials?

Then we need *friendships*. What happens when a leader turns away from lasting friendships? Ours is a mobile society, and it's harder to build friendships on the move. But effective leaders need many friends. I've had the privilege of meeting with a group of associates and close friends for over two decades. Every May, Dorothy and I meet with six of these couples for a weekend together someplace across the country to renew our warm fellowship and acquaintance. For us, anything less would be a form of abandonment.

We need to be *reading*. Millions have left the enduring words of a book for the flickering screen of a television set. But advice, orders, instruction, warning and encouragement all wait on the printed page. I love to read and I love to encourage others to do the same. For example, I've willed my set of the Harvard Classics to one of my grandsons who's an avid reader. But first I'm going through them over the next couple of years myself. I've got the whole set, and I want to see what great writing is. Why be one of those who would leave the collective wisdom of the entire civilized world waiting in the next room for an entire lifetime? Leaders are readers; and readers are leaders.

We mustn't neglect *fellowship*. To neglect fellowship is to neglect the life blood of leadership. Why should anyone follow a leader without knowing positively that that person really cares for his or her needs and well-being? And how can a leader communicate such interest without fellowship? Maybe it's the plain, old-fashioned ice cream social experience. Perhaps it's a formal gathering. Maybe it's a large group, or a small face-to-face encounter. A leader in touch is a leader involved is a leader in control.

And don't forget *dating*. Date your spouse. Never forget to fill his or her life with fond memories. Take a trip. Go shopping. See a good play. *Forget that you're a leader and be a lover.*

These may seem like harmless electives in life. But when a leader ignores the fuels that regenerate personal effectiveness, that leader is walking away from a primary responsibility to self. And you cannot leave yourself without leaving the family that relies upon you.

If you can leave these priorities, there's another related danger. When did you leave your first love? Remember the clarity of your call to be a servant, a witness, a pastor or an evangelist? When did you leave that driving desire to give your best to God? It doesn't happen overnight. It's a gradual thing we all have to guard against.

FAMILY MEMBERS LEFT BEHIND

If the shepherds have difficulty in keeping their family priorities in line, what of the sheep?

Today, it appears that we have a strong bent towards institutionalizing our elderly. We've put the pain aside so we don't have to make priorities out of less than productive members of our family. What a tragedy!

Family decline has become a virtual cliché in modern society. But what are the implications for the future as the years go by and our population ages? The realities of this situation—both for today and for tomorrow—should motivate all Christian leaders to keep their own houses in order.

Life expectancy in 1900 was 47. Today, it's 72 for men and 77 for women. The United States now has 30 million people age 65 and older, 2.5 million of whom are age 80 or more according to Stanley Brody, a gerontologist at the University of Pennsylvania. About 12 percent of the population will be older than 65 by the year 2000 with approximately 5 million of these more than 80 years old.

Although many senior citizens are not significantly disabled, one out of six—more than 5 million people age 65 or older—needs help with such daily activities as bathing, cooking, dressing, grooming and stair climbing. About 1.5 million have five or more of these limitations and require long-term care.

The rapid increase in this functionally limited population has created what experts on aging call "parent care." Many seniors' children in their 40s, 50s and 60s face the dilemma of paying $35,000 a year to place a parent in a qualified nursing home, of putting the parent in a substandard nursing home, or of absorbing the emotional and economic costs of caring for the parent in their own homes according to Robert Binstock, a Case Western Reserve University gerontologist. Many families are quietly going broke.

The average nursing home patient is an 82-year-old

widow who has three or more chronic disabilities. The most common are heart and circulatory diseases, arthritis, rheumatism and diabetes.

A National Academy of Sciences report says 50 percent or more have some mental or behavioral problem, attributable to Alzheimer's disease, depression or psychosis. Many are so demented they cannot express pain or complain of thirst or hunger. Others are isolated by deafness or blindness.

Women in these institutions outnumber men three to one.

In trendsetting California, only 15 percent of those in long-term care are able to walk on their own; 79 percent need help dressing; 86 percent, with bathing, 39 percent, with feeding; and 29 percent, with toilet functions.

Seventy percent of the patients do not have a spouse, and at least one-fourth have no relatives whatsoever. Of those three-fourths who do have relatives, more than half of them received no visitors in a one-year period.

As the years glide into the future, these trends will only intensify. The need for correct priorities starts right at home with a leader's own family members.

PRIORITY PRIMER

1. Take care of your own life before you offer to take care of the lives of others.

2. Serve your own family before serving the family of others.

3. Answer our Seven Selective Questions when placing first things first.

4. Use "Posteriorities" to sort out what you don't want to achieve.

5. Work at ridding yourself of workaholism.

6. Remember the importance of recreation, friendships, reading, fellowship, dating and other true priorities.

7. Prepare now to give priority to aging members of your family.

Throughout this chapter we've examined the importance of well-placed priorities. This skill—the ability to balance the needs of God, family, friends, strangers and self—is one of the final touchstones of a true leader. For without it, leadership is reduced to little more than an endless stream of cold, unfeeling orders.

When did you leave your family behind? No matter what the answer may have been, last year, yesterday or an hour ago, the one reply I'm most anxious to hear is something similar to "Never again!" Without the strong support of our family and friends, you and I cannot face the years ahead with confidence. But with that support, all things become possible. I sincerely hope you are well supplied with this source of strength as we contemplate a scenario for the twenty-first century, the subject of chapter 10.

Chapter Ten

THE FUTURE
A Scenario for the Twenty-First Century

I asked a younger pastor in Minneapolis, "What do your people most need to be mobilized for world evangelism?" He pondered a moment and answered quietly, "A staggering view of God."

> *"The most important ingredient*
> *of the future is the present."*
>
> George Leonard

We opened chapter 1 with a look at several important "torches." Who can forget the excitment of the Olympic Torch relay in 1984? Or who could have missed the majestic new torch on the Statue of Liberty in 1986? But more exciting and majestic than either of these is the torch of truth we Christians uphold throughout the course of time.

What I've shared with you throughout these chapters is a prelude to a far more important relay. The ideas, the experiences, the Scriptures we have shared about leadership all have the potential for helping you seize this brighter torch.

But these principles of leadership don't automatically explain the importance of this torch I offer. What does it really mean? How valuable *is* the one true light?

Maybe those of us passing the torch and those who seize it can run with greater determination if we consider a dark scenario. What would be the consequences if this torch should fall to the ground, its light going out forever? Let's contrast the sinister outcome of failure with the joyous outcome of success in this team effort of passing humanity's most important torch.

SHOVE THY NEIGHBOR

Without the light of a divine Father who created all men as brothers, the plans of Hitler, Idi Amin and Colonel Kaddafi all make sense. "Why put up with anyone who thinks differently? My way is best, so let my enemies perish," they reason. The Khmer Rouge found it convenient to shove their uncooperative neighbors out into the killing fields. There are those who would do the same in South America, Central America, the Caribbean, East Europe, South Africa and elsewhere.

What kind of light is needed in these shadows?

I was impressed some time ago by two African friends of mine who so beautifully exemplify the power of unity. One is a white South African and the other is a black Ugandan. They are Bishop Festo Kivengere of Uganda, whom we met in chapter 6, and Michael Cassidy, a native of South Africa, the founding head of *African Enterprise*. They work together, in spite of the intense friction between white South Africans and black Africans. Yet these men are close friends and they have enjoyed highly successful joint ministries in many parts of the world. I have had the privilege of being with them on many occasions as they ministered together in services and meetings.

I recall one evening when I served as the master of ceremonies at a well attended dinner. Mike and Festo shared in the program. I was sitting between them. Mike's water glass was empty. He was about to get up to speak.

He asked Festo if he might drink the balance of Festo's glass of water. Without thinking of the black/white tensions so rampant in South Africa, Mike finished the water from Festo's glass! For me that symbolic act said it all. They are truly brothers.

This type of relationship is not natural for us human beings. It has to be taught, modeled and spotlighted with the torch of truth.

THROUGH A GLASS DARKLY

Paul mentioned that even Christians "see through a glass, darkly." (1 Cor. 13:12. *KJV*). But what of the godless world?

In 1775 Patrick Henry proclaimed a belief that went down in history beside his other sentiments about "liberty or death." When asked of the future, he replied, "I know of no way of judging the future but by the past." Certainly that is the case for all who reject divine revelation about the future. Isaiah spoke of sinners who "stumble at noon day as in the night" (Isa. 59:10, *KJV*).

God plagued the Egyptians with physical darkness to remind them of their spiritual confusion. He promises to do the same thing once again in the modern world. "And the fifth angel poured out his vial upon the seat of the beast; and his kingdom was full of darkness; and they gnawed their tongues for pain" (Rev. 16:10, *KJV*). This is physical darkness. Imagine the pain of spiritual blackness.

But with the torch of God's Word we know the joy, the clarity and the confidence about our future. "Then your light shall dawn in the darkness, and your darkness shall be as the noonday" (Isa. 58:10)

How could we ever let the light of the gospel grow dim?

DISUNITY

Christ warned against the danger of division. "If a house be divided against itself, that house cannot stand" (Mark 3:25, *KJV*).

Modern humanism, New Age secularism and scientism run wild today along with communism, heresy and other spiritual infections. Such ideologies affect the Body of Christ by creating disunity, disloyalty and rivalries among Christian brothers. And they exact their toll against

---

The Christian accepts the darkness of world conditions, but at the same time is able to relax about the future because the Word of God clearly reveals that God is in control of history and truth.

---

the effective carrying out of the Great Commission. Add to this the lack of clear definition by some evangelical groups and agencies as to goals, strategies, methods and programs that need to be employed to fulfill Christ's command and the problems become further exacerbated.

Look at the issue of Romanism. I'm an admirer of the Pope because of his strong stands on key issues. But far too many Christians look on this man as a symbol of division. In some areas I wish he were more liberal, as was Pope John XXIII. But the obstacle of Papal infallibility is something we *can* resolve with the clear light of truth and cooperation.

Another serious shadow against the profile of the

church is liberation theology. Though filled with Marxist extremism, there's a cry behind the rhetoric of the oppressed masses that needs the serious attention of our new Christian leaders.

Other divisions arise over diverse understanding about the end time. Obviously there are differing views among believers as to eschatology. But certainly there is neither cause nor reason for Christians to despair because ominous clouds envelope our world and threaten total destruction. The increase of evil need not darken our spirits either, for God's righteousness will prevail. "Where sin abounded, grace abounded much more" (Rom. 5:20).

The Christian accepts the darkness of world conditions, but at the same time is able to relax about the future because the Word of God clearly reveals that God is in control of history and truth. The Word clearly teaches that righteousness will triumph. The book of Revelation closes on a victorious note. This does not mean mankind will escape severe judgment, but we know God will vindicate Himself and His faithful followers.

Though great upheavals may sweep the religious world, the biblical Christian has marching orders that must not fail. We cannot escape the truth. God has commissioned us to preach the gospel to the end of history as we may know it. This is part of His plan; for God wills that no individual should perish. It is encouraging to know God is raising up vast numbers of Christians who can, by virtue of His power within, be instruments of hope and salvation amid confusion and despair.

My eschatology is broad. I believe the Lord could come very soon, and I often pray, "even so come, Lord Jesus." But whether it's 1 year, 10, 100, or even a 1,000, our job remains unchanged. We all have but *one lifetime* to serve the Lord.

THE POWER OF UNITY

As Christians our hope for the future is unity. This was never more evident nor clearly manifested than during the days of first believers. Truly this was one of the remarkable features of the early Christian church at Jerusalem. This was true in spite of the great diversity among them. Unity was there because of daily vigilance. The early Christian leaders constantly exhorted the Christian community with this urgent need.

The early church expressed herself in the prevailing view that there was only one church or Body of Christ. Diversity of gifts was recognized, but these believers viewed all Christians as one with each other. This enabled them to minister effectively—so much so that Luke records in Acts 17:6 that they "turned the world upside down."

In Acts this unity was expressed in various ways. It was clearly seen by the depth and warmth of Christian fellowship, both at worship and in their homes. It was expressed by sharing with those less fortunate. The early church welcomed outsiders and outcasts. Their homes were always open to their brothers in the faith.

Some of this may have been a carry-over from Jewish tradition and culture. From childhood, believers were taught a strong social consciousness. The Torah laid great emphasis upon welcoming the stranger and sojourner. The early church was bound together into closely knit families of spiritual fellowship that continually reached out to the needy. The effect of this unity of fellowship was a mighty force for carrying out the church's mission of evangelization.

This emphasis on unity did not cease with the book of Acts. It was also stressed by the Apostles in their writings. But it is nowhere better expressed than by the term that Paul often used, "We are laborers together with God" (1 Cor. 3:9, *KJV*). He was talking about partnership. The apostle addressed himself to this issue on many occasions (see 1 Cor. 12:15,16,21).

This same unity has preserved the Church through Roman persecution, the Dark Ages, industrialization, world wars and the space age. It can also preserve us against the gates of hell, better known as the nuclear age. But the burning question every torchbearer for Christ must answer is, How many unreached peoples will suffer because of our inability to reach the world soon enough?

Are we Christian evangelists doing enough to support each other in the common efffort?

It is an attractive model to see an African, an Asian, and a European working together in evangelism.

Equality, support and mutual acceptance mean we in the West cannot think quite so much of the senior/junior relationship we often adopt when considering fellow Christian workers from other nations. We must use our gifts to supplement and complement each other. This may not necessarily be two people working together. It could be a whole body of leaders and members of the congregation who share in mission, contributing their various gifts. One might have the gift of teaching, another the gift of evangelism, another the gift of administration, another of giving help and support. Whatever the gift, all contribute meaningfully in a partnership which is coequal, even though individual talents and gifts may differ. It would be wrong to attempt to qualify the gifts God has given to us and say one gift is stronger or more important than another. Partnership means everyone who shares in the ministry of evangelism or church growth makes valid and acceptable contributions to the joint ministry according to individual callings.

It is an attractive model to see an African, an Asian, and a European working together in evangelism.

THE MONGOLIAN CONNECTION

Several years before attending the International Congress on World Evangelization at Lausanne, Switzerland in 1974, I had heard a student of world missions say that to our knowledge there were no Christians in Outer Mongolia in northern China. The statement of this fact impressed me and I began praying for people in that part of the world. I had never prayed for them before, having never really thought about that great sweep of land south of Asiatic Russia being in need of The Torch.

At the Lausanne Congress each morning in the large auditorium nearly 4,000 delegates from 150 different nations shared in a Bible study for about 30 minutes. Each day there was a different leader from a different part of the world who brought the Bible message from the book of Acts, illustrating how God had mightily worked in that first century church. One morning the Bible lesson leader might be a European, the next an African, another day an Asian, the next a Latin, until all people had been represented.

Following each of these messages we, as delegates, would gather in small groups of 8 or 10 throughout that great hall to counsel and talk together concerning what we had heard. Then we prayed together for 20 or 25 minutes.

One morning, as my wife, Dorothy, and I were seated in our group, I noticed a distinguished Chinese gentleman. We began getting acquainted in our group and I asked this man for his name and where he came from. With a smile, he said, "I am the only delegate here in this Congress from Outer Mongolia." Immediately I reached across the back of my chair and hugged him. I must have frightened him by such emotion, and I'm certain he didn't know what was happening. Then I told him I had been praying for people in Outer Mongolia and I was thrilled to meet someone from that country. He showed me his Bible, which was in the Mongol language with Chinese characters. He was extremely proud of it because there are very few Bibles available in his language. I asked him what his present responibilities were. He told me he was living in Kaoshuong, in southern Taiwan, and that he was producing a 15-minute radio broadcast each day that was being beamed shortwave from Taiwan into Outer Mongolia. I could hardly believe my ears!

I asked him, "Are there many Christians there now?" He replied, "Oh, yes. There are literally scores, and more people are being converted to Christ all the time." We talked further and he shared with me his anticipation that there would soon be a strong moving of the Spirit of God among his people.

What a thrill for me! Here I thought the people for whom I had been praying were locked behind tightly closed doors. God was so gracious to give me some confirmation of answered prayer by allowing me to meet the only delegate from Mongolia among those thousands of delegates from around the world! Here he was—a fellow torchbearer—in our little group of 10 who prayed together that morning!

And now the Presbyterian and the Evangelical Alliance

Mission radio stations in Seoul, Korea, are beaming the gospel daily by shortwave into Mongolia as well.

This revelation was not the only fruit of that conference in 1974. What was perceived as a single conference of evangelists has now blossomed into a full-fledged international movement, the Lausanne Committee for World Evangelization. It has already has become one of the most influential Christian movements of the twentieth century.

In January of 1987 I had the opportunity to attend a planning conference in Callaway Gardens, Geogia with Dr. Leighton Ford, Chairman of the Lausanne Committee for World Evangelization. Leighton Ford is a close friend and colleague, a man of intelligence, integrity and prayer. His perspective about the organization and his vision for the future are extremely inspirational. For that reason, I would like to share a portion of Dr. Ford's remarks with you. They demonstrate a widening of the trail we all can use in carrying our torch to the world.

LAUSANNE COMMITTEE FOR WORLD EVANGELIZATION
CHAIRMAN'S ADDRESS, JAN. 19, 1987
(CONDENSED)
by Leighton Ford

"What is Lausanne?" Sometimes it seems we are always being asked and asking ourselves what Lausanne is all about. I think it is an important question to be constantly addressed, to understand what God has called us to be. Lausanne is a movement of people in Christ who covenant together for biblical world evangelization.

"We are a movement—not primarily a

structure. We are people in Christ, identified in Him, not primarily by our labels. We focus on world evangelization as primary in the many aspects of the church's mission.

"And, we covenant together—not that we signed a covenant just once in Lausanne, but we regularly re-covenant together for this task to which God has called us.

"As you know, I have left 30 wonderful years spent with Billy Graham and his Association and have launched the Leighton Ford Ministries. Through Leighton Ford Ministries we want to communicate hope in Christ with integrity and creativity and to enable God's people, especially the younger emerging leaders for this task.

"It was 1986 in Oslo during a prayer meeting, that someone quoted words from Scripture that became to me a confirmation and new direction for Lausanne. Clive Calver quoted Isaiah 43:18, 19: 'Remember not the former things; do not dwell on the past, behold I am doing a new thing. Even now it is springing forth. Do you not perceive it?'

"In my judgment, Lausanne is at a transition point, when God is perhaps going to do a new thing. We must always keep our commitment under the covenant, to the gospel, to the Scriptures and the primacy of evangelism. Our gospel and our goal will never change or can never change.

"The Lord reminded His prophet Isaiah how He was the Lord who had made a way in the sea and brought Israel from Egypt. Yet as great as the past was, He told them: do not dwell on the past. Now He was going to do a new thing, make a way in the wilderness and rivers in the desert. God is always doing a new thing. As we respond in faith and obedience, He delivers us not only from old defeats, but from old victories, old habits, old patterns.

"Lausanne has a gift of new leadership. God is doing a new thing also in bringing younger leadership into Lausanne. If the Lausanne movement is to continue after this decade, and I believe that it must, then younger leadership must be brought in at every point and given responsibility. I believe we are at a transition point in Christian leadership throughout the world. Many of our senior, pioneer leaders are coming to the end of their ministries. A new group of creative, gifted younger leaders, forty years of age and under, is also emerging in many parts of the world. I say to you younger leaders: you are not window dressing. You are a gift from God to our movement. We need the fresh wind of your ideas as you also need to know the roots of Lausanne.

"Lausanne is also in a transition time from being a committee to becoming a movement. It's not a movement which wants to control and direct, but one which seeks to enable and to encourage. Lausanne is a web of relationships between evangelistically-concerned leaders in all parts of the world seeking to establish linkages which will enable those with similar evangelistic callings to be more effective.

"As we move into the global information

era, I believe the Lausanne movement is providentially poised by God to be His instrument. Highly organized, hierarchical structures are less and less effective. Loosely organized networks across which information can freely flow back and forth are becoming more and more typical of our world.

"The New World
"We also need God to do a new thing because we are facing a newer world.

"It will be a *larger* world. If you are 50, the world has doubled in your lifetime. By the year 2000 there will be one and one-half billion more people. India will be the biggest country with more than all of Africa and Latin America.

"It will be a *developing* world. Eighty percent of the population will be in developing countries by 2025. Sixty percent will be in Asia.

"It will be an *older* world. By 2025 there will be one billion people over 60 — one in every 7.

"It will also be a *younger* world. Sixty percent are now under 24. Half of Latin America is under 18. Mexico City has a population under 14 equal to New York City. There is not a Third World city with a median age over 20.

"It will be an *urban* world. Mexico City will have 31 million by the year 2000. By 2000 there will be 22 mega cities, with ten million plus.

"It will certainly be a world of *conflict*. Fifty percent of our scientific minds are engaged in so-called "defense". Many fully expect a nuclear terrorist incident or one between the new nuclear nations by 2000.

"It will be the world of the *"information era"*. A world divided not between haves and have-nots, but between knows and know-nots. We can now send the Encyclopedia Brittanica across the Atlantic six times a minute. If the auto industry kept up with computer information advance, a Rolls-Royce would get 3 million miles a gallon, would cost less than $3 and you could put six on the head of a pin. Jean Pierre du Prie, an information specialist, said, "The more we 'communicate' the way we do, the more we create a hellish world. Ours is a world about which we pretend to have more information, yet one that is increasingly void of meaning."

"And it will be a different world in *religion*. Islam is growing 16 percent a year; Hinduism is growing 12 percent, Buddhism 10 percent, Christianity 9 percent. There are now more Muslims than Baptists in Britain. Yet David Barrett speaks of the era of 'universal response' and 'global access'.

"By 2000 the number of missionaries from Africa, Latin America and Asia may exceed North America's.

"Yet the younger churches may well need revival and renewal from nominalism.

"North America and Europe will be seen increasingly as spiritually bankrupt for all our success, technology and Hedonism.

"What Do We Need Most?

"I asked a younger pastor in Minneapolis: 'What do your people most need to be mobilized for world evangelism?' He pondered a moment and answered quietly: 'a staggering view of God.' As we face this great, growing, suffering surging world; as we face the vast dimensions of world evangelism; as we face the programs before us in the next several years, I am convinced that only a 'staggering view of God' will be enough to take us through.

"As our Lausanne Sr. Associate, Ray Bakke has traveled the cities of the world, and has asked the leaders in his consultations to list the obstacles to reaching their cities with the gospel of Christ. Inevitably, he says, seven of the ten reasons are internal to the church—not external to the world—lack of vision, lack of prayer, lack of unity, lack of talent, leadership, too busy to spend time with non-Christians—these are the typical problems.

"As Archbishop William Temple said years ago, 'The evangelization of those without cannot be separated from the re-kindling of devotion of those within.'

"Judgment must always begin with the house of God. Twelve years ago the Lausanne Covenant called us not to be triumphant, but to be penitent. The Lord complained in Isa. 42:19, 'Who is blind but my servant? or deaf as my messenger that I sent?' Then he said that he had 'poured out his anger' upon his people who had not followed his ways.

"Perhaps our greatest need today in the church worldwide is a recovery of true, biblical holiness. Robert McShane said, 'My people's greatest need is . . . . ' What would you say? McShane said, 'my personal holiness.'

"In Scripture God says, 'Be ye holy as I am holy.' He doesn't ask us to be strong as He is or all-knowing as He is. He does ask us to be holy as He is. The pursuit of holiness, I think, is a neglected priority in our Christian mission strategy.

"So what a tremendous reassurance when the God who pours out His anger on our disobedience also promises to pour out His spirit for our obedience. Isa. 44:3 'For I will pour water upon him that is thirsty, and floods upon the dry ground: I will pour my spirit upon thy seed and my blessing upon thine offspring.'

"I am afraid too many of us, especially in the West today, want a Christ without a cross, a Savior who will fulfill us, but not call us to suffering. Yet we are called not just to receive Jesus as Savior, but to follow Him as Lord and the way of the cross."[1]

I am grateful to Dr. Leighton Ford and the Lausanne Committee for their tireless efforts in setting the pace for this torch relay of world evangelism. They are helping thousands of believers and thousands of congregations multiply the power of individual faith.

WHEN MEN PRAYED AND THE WORLD WAS CHANGED

It happened during a very dark period in American history, the Great Depression. A group of laymen in Charlotte, North Carolina became deeply burdened for their city's spiritual condition. They took off work to pray—no small sacrifice in those hard times. Meeting in the early morning in a farmhouse, they began to pray for revival in their city. As the day passed, their faith grew and they prayed, "Lord, do something in our city that will touch our whole state and nation and even the world!"

Could they possibly have dreamed how their prayers would be answered? The next year they held an evangelistic campaign and one of the farmer's teenage sons came forward and took up the torch of Christ. His name was Billy Graham.

Among Billy Graham's many accomplishments was the formation of the Lausanne Committee in 1974. He recently issued a list of 10 challenges to this organization for the decades ahead. I found them as powerful as they are informative. The following were published in the December 1986 issue of *World Evangelization:*

10-Point Challenge

1. The challenge of reaching the unreached in the next generation.
2. The challenge of creatively using technology to reach the world.
3. The challenge of preserving evangelistic gains by laying a theological base committed to the authority of an infallible Scripture.
4. The challenge of a steadily growing prayer base.
5. The challenge of the bold evangelization of nominal Christians in the West.
6. The challenge of supporting and training Spirit-gifted evangelists.
7. The clear declaration of the evangelistic mission of Lausanne based on the Lausanne Covenant.

8. The challenge of remaining a para-church movement—open to the world but exclusively evangelical.
9. The challenge of building a financial support base founded upon popular prayer support.
10. The challenge of unswerving support of evangelical movements and churches worldwide that lovingly but firmly resist biblical heresy and error.[2]

If met, these challenges could shake the world for good—whether accomplished through the Lausanne Committee for World Evangelization, through a local committee for church missions, or through one's own personal witnessing for Christ. And for those of us who have served the Master for most of our lifetime, such challenges afford an opportunity to pass the torch of God's truth along to a new generation of leaders.

We have shared several stirring occasions when the whole world shouted, "Look at the torch." All eyes turned to the Olympic Torch in '84 and the Statue of Liberty's torch in '86. To what will they look in the years that usher in the twenty-first century?

Now you who read this book have the opportunity to do far more than merely look at the torch. You are permitted to seize it and run. Think what a disappointment and tragedy it would have been had the Olympic torch fallen to the ground and gone out. Think how all the world would have gasped if some terrorist had sabotaged the lighting of the torch of liberty at Ellis Island in 1986. How much more of a catastrophe would it be if the next generation God has prepared to bear *His* torch were to let it fall to the ground, die out or be destroyed by the adversary?

You have a golden opportunity to change this society for *good*. It's my prayer that through this book you have discovered—or rediscovered—the needed tools and seen them in action.

TORCH IN REVIEW

1. Commit yourself to God. He wants to share the privilege and joy of carrying His Word.
2. Set your goal on the next runner. Miraculously we bear not one, but untold thousands of torches. Like feeding the five thousand, the more we hand out, the more we have to share.
3. Be motivated by the things that motivate God.
4. Open your heart to God and He will fill it with genuine *enthusiasm*.
5. Live in honesty. They who receive the torch from you must be willing to believe you when you speak of its importance.
6. Be strong and of good courage. Though the night be dark, you will always walk in light when bearing this torch.
7. Decide to decide. Indecision is inaction is failure. Hold out your hand and seize the torch.
8. Act responsibly. You are the hope of more people than you know.
9. Keep first things first.
10. Respect the future. He who "inhabits eternity" invites you to share His home there with Him (see Isa. 57:15).

My final prayer for you, my friend, is: first, submit yourself to God as a willing servant; second, commit yourself to make a difference; and third, never settle for anything mediocre or second best. God is the best and He expects His followers to be the same.

This prayer is not mine alone. It is also the prayer of hundreds of servants who have carried God's torch for many decades. Now the time has come for us to pass it along to you.

Look at the torch. It is yours to carry. Though at times you may stumble and fall, we who hand you this prize are confident you will snap the tape at the finish line with a great and triumphant burst of victory.

May God be with you always.

Notes

Chapter 1
1. From the article "Growing Pains at 40," *Time, May 19, 1986, p. 23.*
2. Ibid.
3. From *Success* magazine, April 1985, pp. 55, 56.
4. Ted W. Engstrom with Robert C. Larson, *A Time for Commitment* (Grand Rapids, MI: Zondervan Publishing House, 1987).
5. From the *Global Prayer Digest,* U.S. Center for World Missions, May 1984.

Chapter 2
1. D. Marquis (1878-1937), American humorist.
2. Ted W. Engstrom, "Impressions of a Christian Serviceman," *Moody Monthly,* July 1944; *The Alliance Weekly,* August 1944.
3. Frank Goble, *Excellence in Leadership* (Ottawa, IL: Green Hill Publishers, 1978), p. 128-130.
4. Alan Lakein, *How to Get Control of Your Time and Your Life* (New York: New American Library, 1974).
5. Ted W. Engstrom and Alex Mackenzie, *Managing Your Time* (Grand Rapids: Zondervan Publishing House, 1967).
6. David Barrett, World Christian Encyclopedia: *A Comparative Survey of Churches and Religions in the Modern World, A.D. 1900 to 2000* (New York: Oxford University Press, 1982).
7. John Perkins, *With Justice for All* (Ventura, CA: Regal Books, 1982).
8. Herbert Kane, *Understanding Christian Missions* (Grand Rapids, MI: Baker Books, 1986), p. 338.
9. Ibid., p. 334.

Chapter 3
1. William James (1842-1910), American philosopher.
2. Ted W. Engstrom, *The Making of a Christian Leader* (Grand Rapids, MI: Zondervan Publishing House, 1976), p. 67.
3. Ted W. Engstrom and Alex Mackenzie, *Managing Your Time* (Grand Rapids: Zondervan Publishing House, 1967), p. 133.
4. From *Robert H. Schuller Tells You How to Be an Extraordinary Person in an*

Ordinary World by Robert H. Schuller, copyright 1985 by Robert A. Schuller. Used by permissino of Fleming H. Revell Company.
5. From *Newsweek* magazine, Oct. 9, 1986, p. 44.
6. Schuller, *Extraordinary Person.*

Chapter 4
1. Jim Petersen, *Evangelism As a Life-style* (Colorado Springs, CO: Navpress, 1980). Used by permission.
2. Dale Carnegie, *How to Stop Worrying and Start Living* (New York: Pocket Books, Div. of Simon & Schuster, Inc., 1984).
3. John Gardener, *Excellence* (New York: Norton, 1987).
4. Og Mandino, *Og Mandino's University of Success* (New York: Bantam, 1982), p. xiii.
5. Ordway Tead, *The Art of Leadership* (New York: McGraw-Hill Book Co., Inc., 1963), pp. 289-299. Used by permission.
6. Ibid., p. 125.
7. Frank Goble, *Excellence in Leadership* (Ottawa, IL: Green Hill Publishers, 1978).
8. From "A Vision for Evangelizing the Real America," *International Bulletin of Missionary Research,* April 1986, pp. 59-64.
9. Ibid.

Chapter 5
1. Reprinted with permission of Green Hill Publishers, Inc. from *Excellence in Leadership* by Frank Goble, $8.95 paperback.
2. Robert Samuelson, "The Super Bowl of Scandal," *Newsweek,* Dec. 1, 1986, p. 64.
3. Ibid., p. 48.
4. Paddy Calistro, "Shifting the Weight," *Los Angeles Times* magazine, Nov. 30, 1986, p. 38.
5. Horace L. Fenton as quoted in the *Latin American Evangelist,* 1971.

Chapter 6
1. Thomas Carlyle (1795-1881), Scottish historian.
2. Festo Kivengere, *I Love Idi Amin* (Old Tappan, NJ: Fleming H. Revell, 1977).
3. Beverly Beyette, "NOW's Birthday More than a Nostalgia Trip," *Los Angeles Times,* Nov. 23, 1986, Part VI, p. 14.
4. Taken from the *Pasadena Star News,* Dec. 16, 1986.
5. Erwin Lutzer, "The Myths that Could Destroy America," *The Rebirth of America* (USA: Arthur S. DeMoss Foundation, 1986), p. 84.
6. Beth Spring and Kelsey Menehan, "Women in Seminary: Preparing for What?" *Christianity Today,* Sept. 5, 1986, p. 18.
7. Ibid., p. 22.
8. Roberta Hestenes, *The Next Step: Women in a Divided Church* (Waco, TX: Word Books, 1987).

Chapter 7
1. Adolphe Monod (1802-1856) French theologian.
2. Ted W. Engstrom, *Your Gift of Administration* (Nashville, TN: Thomas Nelson, Inc., 1983).

253
E588

96242

LINCOLN CHRISTIAN COLLEGE AND SEMINARY

3. Ibid., p. 76.
4. From Donald G. Bloesch, "Secular Humanism—Not the Only Enemy," *Eternity*, Jan. 1982, p. 22.

Chapter 8
1. Peter Drucker, contemporary author.
2. Frank Goble, *Excellence in Leadership* (Ottawa, IL: Green Hills Publisher, 1978).
3. Excerpt from *The Practice of Management* by Peter F. Drucker. Copyright 1954 by Peter F. Drucker. Reprinted by permission of Harper & Row, Publishers, Inc.
4. Ibid.
5. From "Mainline to Sideline," *Newsweek*, Dec. 22, 1986, p. 54.
6. Ibid., p. 55.
7. C. Peter Wagner, "A Vision for Evangelizing the Real America," *International Bulletin Missionary Research*, April 1986, p. 64.

Chapter 9
1. Martin Luther King., Jr. (1929-1968), American clergyman and civil rights leader.
2. C. Peter Wagner, "Confessions of a Workaholic," *Eternity*, Aug. 1975, Vol. XXVI, No. 8. Reprinted by permission of *Eternity* magazine, copyright 1987, Evangelical Ministries, Inc., 1716 Spruce Street, Philadelphia, PA 19103.
3. Ibid.
4. Ibid.
5. John R.W. Stott, *Balanced Christianity* (Downers Grove, IL: InterVarsity Press, 1975).

Chapter 10
1. Used by permission of Dr. Leighton Ford.
2. Billy Graham, *World Evangelization*, Dec. 1986, p. 3.

3 4711 00148 6689